Perfume

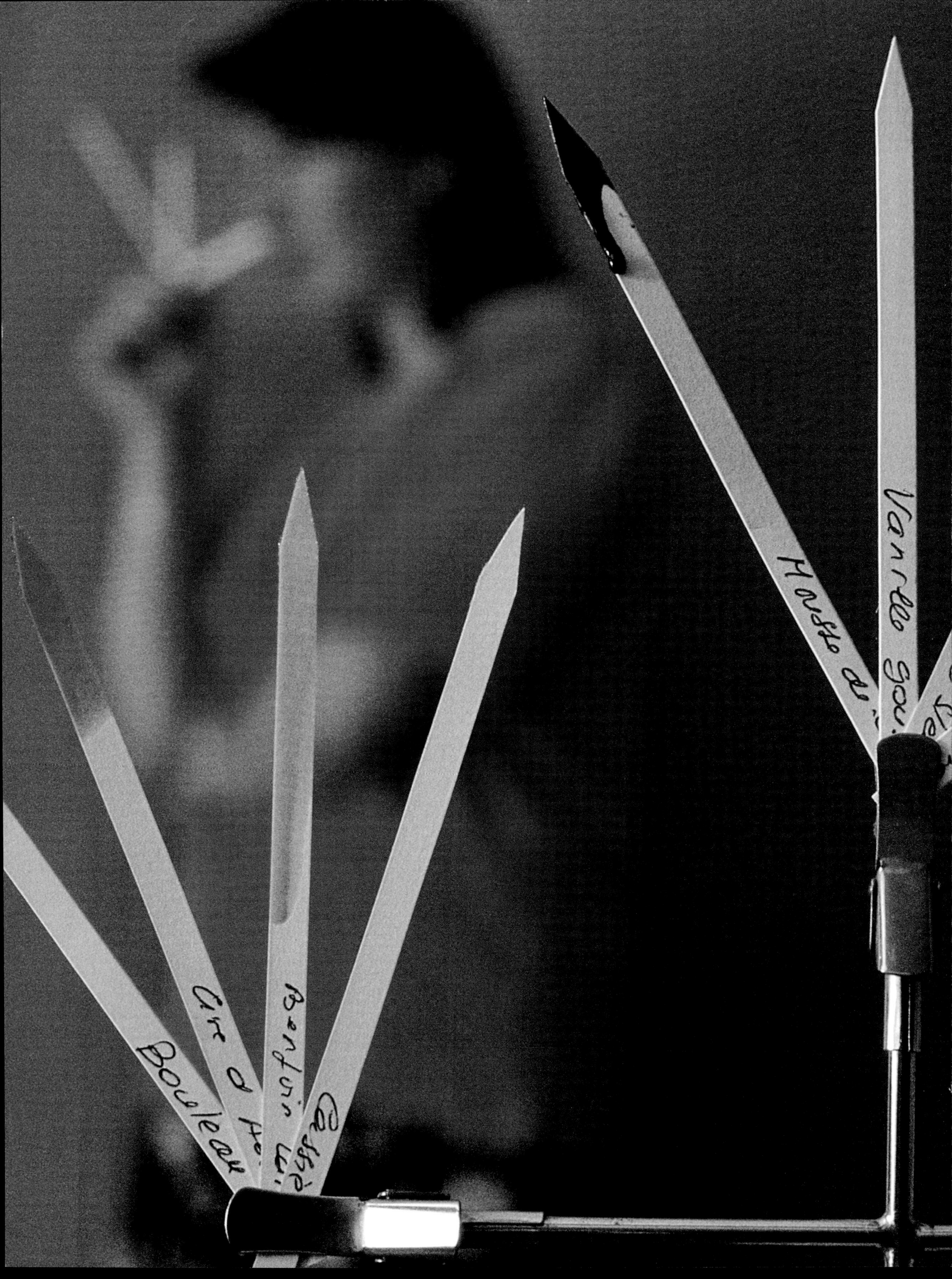
Bouleau

Perfume

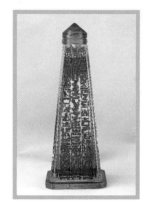

THE ART AND SCIENCE OF SCENT

Cathy Newman

Photography by
Robb Kendrick

NATIONAL GEOGRAPHIC SOCIETY

For Jim and Jeb
—C.N.

To Jeannie and Gus,
who endure my time
away from home with patience
and support.
—R.K.

Newman, Cathy.
    Perfume : the art and science of scent / Cathy Newman;
photography by Robb Kendrick.
        p.   cm.
    Includes index.
    ISBN 0-7922-7378-8
    1. Perfumes.   I. Title.
TP983.N45   1998
668'.54—dc21   98-23082

        CIP

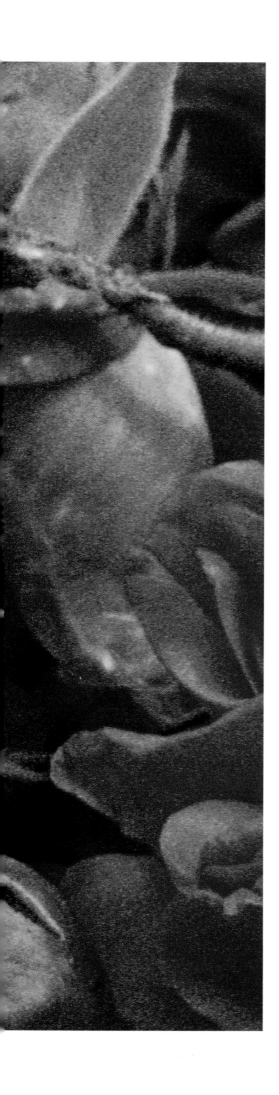

C O N T E N T S

WITHDRAW

A Passion for Jasmine

I fell in love with fragrance in an unlikely setting—a warehouse-like metal shed filled with steam, pipes, and metal vats. I was in a factory near Grasse, France, where flowers are processed for oil, and Joseph Mul, owner of 25 acres of jasmine and rose fields, was taking me through a highly technical, and to my mind, tedious process called chemical extraction. It was dark and drab in the factory, and I itched to escape to the luminescent landscape outside. Finally Mul finished talking and pulled out a small tin filled with a waxy solid. He waved it teasingly under my nose, then looked at me expectantly.

At first I didn't smell a thing. In fact, I wondered if I was supposed to. Perhaps he was pulling my leg? Was he testing me? Then, as the essence was warmed by his hand, the fragrance lifted and I caught my first hint of French jasmine.

Some things are beyond words, and the scent of French jasmine is one of them. It was heavenly. I doubt I will ever smell anything so lush again.

I had, by then, spent countless hours in corporate offices in New York and Paris listening to discourses on market strategy, globalization, and brand support—the company ploy of spending big money on advertising and marketing to keep the name of their fragrance in the public eye and mind. I had learned fragrance industry jargon. "Juice" was slang for the scent in the bottle. "Doors" was shorthand for the stores where the "product" was sold. "Shipped out" meant how many boxes of product left the factory, as opposed to "sell through," which meant how many bottles actually sold.

The scent of jasmine reminded me what this

A fragrant cloud of jasmine cradles the head of Sylvio Suquet, who until recently grew and harvested a small plot of the flowering plant near Grasse, France. French jasmine is one of the costliest fragrances in perfumery.

story was about. It was, among other things, about magic.

It was a magic, I would discover, that could take many forms. The perfumers were the wizards; the perfume itself was a wand. A perfume could, if one bought into the illusion, transform a person into someone prettier, sexier, and more charming. Fragrance could also erase boundaries of time and place. That was another magic. A whiff of Vent Vert, my mother's "summer perfume," conjured her presence with an immediacy that took my breath away.

But let me backtrack. This book began as a magazine piece for NATIONAL GEOGRAPHIC. It was to be a thorough, yet contained trip through the process of creating fragrance. It would take the reader from the flower in the field to the flacon on the department store counter. Instead, the story stretched into a year-long inquiry that spilled over the confines of a magazine and into the book you hold.

In the course of my exploration I would hear many stories about how fragrance could reach into the cave of the heart. But nothing would prickle my skin like the story one perfumer told me about the memories unleashed by the smell of his father's cologne. A bottle of that cologne sat on the desk in front of him. He lifted the cap off and the scent of his father's fragrance filled the air. It was as if his long-dead father had materialized in the room. The moment was powerful and heart-bruising.

Some memories were less complicated. "Do you know if they still make Bellodgia by Caron?" an older gentleman once asked me. (They do.)

"It was worn by the first girlfriend I was cozy with," he explained with old-fashioned tact.

And so the scent of French jasmine would be filed in my own archive as resonant of all that was beautiful and precious about perfume. I would, throughout my journey in the realm of fragrance, hold fast to that memory, returning to it from time to time as I would to a talisman.

I found out that Joseph Mul owned what was perhaps the last large field of jasmine in France. French jasmine, it seemed, was extraordinarily rare. In fact, it was rarer than French truffles. Mul's entire harvest of flowers added up to scarcely 22 tons. That was it—the sum total of the world production of French jasmine.

I learned perfume arithmetic. Those 22 tons of petals produced less than 75 pounds of concentrate, known as an *absolue*. At $12,000 a pound, Mul's *absolue jasmin de Grasse* was too expensive for all but a few of the most expensive and prestigious perfumes. So perfumers used jasmine from India, priced at a mere $500 a pound. Or they turned to synthetic jasmine compounds at $16 a pound.

So I could track the economic shifts and progress (if one wished to call it that) of the fragrance industry through this delicate, white, star-shaped flower. The essence of jasmine—its beauty, its preciousness, its ephemerality— seemed symbolic of the essence of perfume.

The scent of French jasmine also taught me about quality. In Grasse, at a school for perfumers where I learned some of the basics, I was taught to distinguish between French jasmine and its less costly counterparts from India and Egypt. It was an arcane skill to be sure, but I was proud to master it. I read that "the odor of jasmine is unique and . . . cannot be exactly imitated at present . . . by any known synthetic." Having sampled the real thing, I could agree.

"You are going to see the Mul family. *C'est magique*," said an industry executive before my visit to the fields. "It will be the end of it soon, and it will be the end of everything. You cannot replace quality. There is the very good cigar. The very good cashmere. The very good wine. In Santo Domingo the cigar is not as good as Havana. The fabric in Hong Kong is not as good as London. The wine in California is not as good as French Bordeaux," he said.

Like the very good cigar, cashmere, and wine, the cultivation of French jasmine remained a craft. Ten years ago a tractor replaced Bijou and Mignon, the two draft horses that had dutifully plowed Mul's fields. But the flowers themselves defied mechanization. They are still picked by hand, one by one, and placed in special baskets made from chestnut splints, contoured to fit comfortably against the harvester's waist. I liked the idea that the world of fragrance still had room for a basket made for no other purpose than to hold jasmine.

Although Mul, in his sturdy overalls and cloth cap, seemed far removed from the pin-striped suits and silk ties of the corporate world, I learned not to underestimate his rustic savvy. He loved his jasmine plants, but it was, after all, a business. If there was more money to be made growing something else, too bad for jasmine. Or, perhaps, one day French jasmine would be too

expensive for the few perfumes that still used it and those companies would no longer be willing to foot the bill. A development might sprout where flowers once grew. *C'est la vie.*

Yet Mul's affection for the flower was genuine. "There's something special about jasmine. It's velvety and soft," he said almost tenderly, as he showed me his jasmine fields after we had finished our factory tour. A stiff wind tousled the spindly bushes, which stood only a foot and a half high. They would grow another foot or so before flowering. Summer and the harvest were still several months away.

"What do you think about when the jasmine blooms and you can smell the first flowers of the harvest?" I asked, convinced his answer would have the shimmer of poetry.

"I think," Mul said without pause, "we have one hundred days of hard work ahead."

And there it was—even in the jasmine fields of Provence—the two sides of the fragrance industry. There was the gorgeousness of the fragrance itself, but there was also the economic reality and cynicism. It was a tension I was to struggle with throughout the story.

"Business is business," the vice president of a cosmetics company commented in response to a question. Her reply came couched in such a cold, hard voice that I felt reproached, as diminished as a school child. I would be reminded often: Business *is* business.

Much later I spoke with a scientist who had an extraordinary passion for and appreciation of perfume. I had enjoyed my seat on the sidelines of the fragrance industry, I told him. But didn't he find the circus of hype that surrounded this exquisite thing called perfume somewhat disturbing?

"I get so frustrated sometimes that I lose track of the beauty of it all, too," he agreed. "But then it hits me again when I smell Mitsouko or some such perfume."

Whenever I lost track of the beauty, the memory of French jasmine set me straight. Even after my return to Washington, the fragrance haunted me. As a graduation present the director of the perfumery school I had attended gave me a blotter dipped in French jasmine. She had wrapped it carefully in plastic and explained that the scent would last for weeks. True to her word, it did. Every so often, as I sat at my desk, I would pull it out of its plastic sleeve, sniff it, and be transported back to Mul's fields. But one day I discovered that the scent had faded. I felt sad. A bit of loveliness had evaporated from my world.

I began to dream about returning to Grasse. Hadn't the director of the perfumery school, a *Grassoise* herself, told me to come for the harvest? September would be best, she advised. At night the wind swept down from the hills; it had once carried the scent of jasmine clear down to Cannes. Nothing could equal the experience of seeing and smelling this for myself, the woman said. Besides, who knew for how much longer Mul would be growing jasmine?

"You must come for the harvest," she repeated. Her eyes brimmed with tears and her voice was filled with emotion. As she spoke the intensity of her feeling touched something in me.

The perfumer must have passion, I heard repeatedly. Fragrance and passion seemed inseparable: Fragrance elicited passion; fragrance was a passion. I had met collectors passionate about perfume bottles; businessmen passionate about the hurly-burly of marketing fragrance; and perfumers passionate about creating fragrance. Now, I realized, I had come away from my exploration into fragrance with a passion of my own: a longing for the scent of *absolue jasmin de Grasse*. My journey had ended, but the invitation to see the harvest was irresistible—a siren song I couldn't ignore.

"Yes," I said, "I will come for the harvest."

The art of the bottle: a flacon created by the French artist Julien Viard around 1923 for a perfume named Femme Divine by Parfums Loulette features clear and frosted crystal with gilded flowers.

The Cathy Perfume

"Do you think of yourself as sensual or elegant?" Cathleen Montrose asks, pen poised over a yellow legal pad.

I'm in an office high above Madison Avenue in New York. Montrose, vice president of creative development for Firmenich, a supplier, or company that creates scents for houses like Calvin Klein Cosmetics and the Estée Lauder Companies, is about to shepherd me through the process of fragrance creation.

"Elegant," I say, glancing down at a run in my stocking.

"What colors do you wear?"

"Black," I reply.

"And?"

"Off-black."

"And?"

"Navy."

A hard look.

Suddenly I'm babbling away. "I'd rather sit with a book than attend a party. If I could afford them, I'd buy emeralds not diamonds. I prefer the ocean to mountains, and I can't stand suffocating florals."

"NO TUBEROSE," Montrose scribbles.

The monologue resumes. "Given a choice I'd wear Yves Saint Laurent, not that fussy Christian Lacroix (noting my chewed fingernails). I prefer red wine to white (inspecting ink stain on hand), and I love John Singer Sargent portraits—especially 'Madame X'. I adore 'Madame X'," I say.

I take a deep breath. "I'd like an understated perfume. Sparkling. Sophisticated. Witty."

The confession will be distilled into what's known in the fragrance business as a brief—an outline of the perfume's concept and target customer (Generation X, Ladies Who Lunch, or, in this case, me). The brief ("A fragrance that does not shout; elegant, crisp, sophisticated," it reads.) will be handed to five Firmenich perfumers, each of whom will create a "Cathy" perfume. I will be expected to choose my favorite.

If I were a huge company like Christian Dior Perfumes, the process would be much the same. It begins with the brief, which is commissioned by a cosmetic or household and personal product company to suppliers such as Firmenich, Givaudan Roure, Quest International, Takasago, or International Flavors & Fragrances (IFF), who enter what amounts to a high-stakes horse race. In addition to perfumes, suppliers also create fragrances for household products like

In a progression from plant to perfume, ingredients like clary sage oil are harvested, distilled, mixed, and packaged in a process that ends in a beautiful bottle of fragrance on the department store counter.

detergents and soaps. The fine fragrance business is centered in New York and Paris, but major suppliers have offices around the world to serve an international clientele.

I'm invited to return in two weeks, on March 14, for the first round of submissions. I leave, and in my head a light bulb clicks on: I've created a fantasy of myself.

Emeralds, red wine, Yves Saint Laurent. *Right.* I grew up on Miami Beach, Florida, where a fashion statement was a clear plastic handbag trimmed with seashells and the nearest thing to wine on the table was seltzer. I've been seduced by a never-ever-to-be image. I've heard the siren song of glamour and I'm humming along.

"Perfume," says Sophia Grojsman, IFF's star perfumer, "is a promise in a bottle."

We want to believe. We crave to be prettier, richer, sexier, and happier than we are. "Aspirational" the industry calls it. Perfume speaks more to our vulnerabilities than to our strengths. Consider the labels on the fragrances we buy: Joy, Dolce Vita, Pleasures, Beautiful, White Diamonds, Allure.

As Charles Revson, the cosmetics czar who in 1973 created Charlie, the first American lifestyle perfume, said, "We sell hope."

And we buy. Last year's worldwide sales of fragrance topped 15 billion dollars, more than six billion dollars in the United States alone.

The silver-tongued industry that conjures these dreams is part circus and part creative magic, with smoke and mirrors galore. (Indeed, the word perfume can be traced back to the Latin words *per*, through, and *fumare*, to smoke. The first perfumes were incense: an unfurling plume of hope directed at the gods.)

"It's an industry of myths," said Allan Mottus, a publisher and consultant to the fragrance industry. "It does not hold up under the scrutiny of daylight."

We sat in a coffee shop off Union Square in New York as Mottus recounted stories of hit perfumes: "Giorgio was done on a wing and a prayer, a toll-free number, a magazine scent strip, and went off the charts." He spoke about

flops: "If you've got a dog, you can't dress it up and take it to a dance. What's more, a bad fragrance can take down a company." He mentioned arrogance: "Someone has a hit, then everyone else says, 'I can do that.'" He illustrated the pervasiveness of absurdity: "Take the Italian season, 1993. Procter and Gamble had Laura Biagiotti's Venezia. Unilever had Vendetta. L'Oreal had Giò. Lauder came out with Tuscany Per Donna. It got ugly fast. When it was over, 60 million dollars had been spent, with only one moderate success to show for it all." He recalled family feuds: "Guerlain was a bunch of octogenerians fighting one another. Hell, they'll be better under new management. (In 1994 the French luxury goods conglomerate LVMH Moët Hennessy Louis Vuitton bought out the family.) You can't live on Shalimar."

Call it the usual parade of human folly in pursuit of the next big blockbuster hit. "It's a lot like show business." Mottus sighed.

Two weeks later I return to Firmenich, and Cathleen Montrose hands me a cardboard box with a clutch of different small spray bottles of fragrance. The labels bear enticing names like Blue Iris, Mirage, and Tempest, conferred on them by the perfumers. My greedy impulse is to spray them all on at once, but Cathleen says that I should wear one each day and keep a perfume diary so that I may record my reaction to each of the candidate fragrances. "Don't try and smell more than three in a row, anyway," she warns, and shows me how to execute the perfumer's equivalent of clearing the palate. "After you've smelled several, sniff the sleeve of your jacket to clear your nose," she instructs. "Then you'll be able to sample more fragrances."

The perfumers are full of advice as well. Annie Buzantian, creator of Mirage, explains that you really can't get an idea whether a perfume works until you wear it. "Like the difference between a dress on the hanger and a dress on your body."

Harry Frémont, who has submitted Voyages and Wraparound, says the first impression is often the right one. "You can overthink a perfume," he tells me.

Each day I wear one fragrance. At night I record my thoughts.

Annie's perfume, Mirage, is inspired by "Madame X," the John Singer Sargent painting I've singled out as a favorite. In the painting an elegant woman in a long, black velvet and satin dress, with fin de siècle ivory skin, stands center stage by a small mahogany side table. Her face turns away from the viewer. Her profile is exquisite. Her stance suggests that she knows it. She is gazing at something, someone—perhaps even nothing.

Montrose interprets for me. "It's the woman as observer, at the same time as being observed. Like you when you're in the field covering a story."

The perfume Annie creates, based on a wild rose scent, is as elegant as the woman in the portrait. I write: *What I imagine an Edith Wharton heroine wearing. Think Newport mansions and garden conservatories. But it's not me. This dress doesn't fit. The perfume is too heady. Almost too romantic. Too fuscia. Too rich. I feel like an imposter. (My problem, not Annie's. I'll never be Madame X.)*

"We all have something inside we wish we can be, but don't dare," Annie tells me later when I confess my misgivings.

Harry Frémont decides to submit two fragrances, Voyages and Wraparound, to reflect the split between my professional and personal lives. Voyages for Cathy, the writer who travels to foreign lands. ("It's about contrasts and the impressions you get while traveling," he says. "The sun and its warmth contrasted with the cold of the sea.") Wraparound for Cathy, the returning mother and wife. ("I envision this as the perfume you wear when you return to your family from a trip abroad.")

I'm not swept away by Voyages. It's a lovely idea, but the scent itself overwhelms. It's too heavy a dose of gardenia and jasmine. *Too warm. I feel like I'm sitting inside of a gardenia bush, instead of just passing by,* I write in my diary.

But Wraparound, with its sandalwood and vanilla lushness, intrigues me. The idea of a perfume that takes care of me is enchanting; wearing it pulls me farther into the perfume-as-security-blanket illusion. *As soothing as a cashmere shawl,* I note. *Can a perfume sing a lullaby? This one almost does. But something strikes me as too sweet. Could some of that be muted. More of a matte finish on the gold?*

During my visit to Firmenich to collect the submissions, Thierry Wasser, a tall, young, Swiss-born perfumer, had explained his fragrance while emphatically expressing his hate for flowers. "You're not going for a walk in the rain forest with this one," he said, shooting me an intense look. He calls his fragrance Metaphor. The name is irresistible to me, of course. Metaphors are a writer's currency. "It's a yin-yang fragrance," Thierry said as he reached over his desk to spray my wrist. "It has two stages: conscious—the orange, mint, and freesia, and unconscious—the Lapsang tea, oakmoss, and tobacco." Whatever is in it soothes. I drifted off and lapsed into a reverie as Thierry spoke about the psychological and emotional overtones of the relationship between perfumer and client. "I am like a shrink for the customer," he said.

After a day of wearing Metaphor, I write in my perfume diary: *By turns exotic and hypnotic. Like a walk through the Cairo souk. Dream-like. This is the fragrance I want to write in. Not a perfume to wear to be noticed. Something different. As if the perfumer had tried to understand me in some deep, searching way. Unnerving, if it weren't so beguiling. I know he hates flowers, but what if there were just a slight hint of floral. Jasmine tea, perhaps?*

I mail my comments to Cathleen Montrose, embarrassed by my fussiness. This one too sweet; that one too dry. Another too strong. Does my fickleness offend the perfumers? Of course not, Montrose says, when we talk. Their job is to please the client.

PRECEDING PAGES The romance of perfume begins in places like the Valley of Roses, near the town of Kazanluk in Bulgaria, where flowers are harvested for their oil. FOLLOWING PAGES The species known as Rosa damascena, when distilled, will provide the heady, intoxicating scent of Bulgarian rose oil worth $4,000 a pound.

Annie Buzantian, a perfumer with Firmenich, samples a fragrance in the company's New York City laboratory. "I never show a client a perfume that isn't beautiful," she says. Firmenich, known in the fragrance industry as a supplier, creates scents for companies such as Christian Dior and Calvin Klein Cosmetics.

In the carefully calibrated world of chemistry, a fragrance is a mix of oils and other additives in a 75 to 95 percent alcohol solution. Perfumes have a concentration of oils greater than 22 percent. *Eau de parfum* has a 15 to 22 percent concentration. The less heady *eau de toilette*, 8 to 15 percent. The even more dilute cologne, less than 5 percent. (The Cathy perfume, the brief specifies, will have a concentration of 15 percent, making it an *eau de parfum*.) The heart of a fragrance lies in the fraction of oils that evaporate off the skin, hit the sensors in the lining of the nose, shoot up the olfactory bulb, and pluck a chord of delight in the mind.

An average fragrance has 60 to 100 ingredients; more complex ones can have 300. Estée Lauder's Beautiful may hold the record with 700. The formula is 12 pages long. But nobody at the Estée Lauder Companies will ever see the formula for Beautiful, just as I will never get my hands on the formula for Mirage, Metaphor, Wraparound, or any of the other Cathy perfumes being worked on. In the dead-bolt secret world of the fragrance industry such information is the sole property of the supplier.

"The ownership of the fragrance remains that of the creator," explains Geoffrey Webster, president of fragrances worldwide at Givaudan Roure, another supplier. "The client is obligated to buy all the fragrance he needs from the supplier for the lifetime of the product."

What's to prevent a company from pulling a fast one by analyzing the formula, then having someone else duplicate and produce it more cheaply?

Nothing really, but it almost never happens, says Webster. "Relationships between perfumers and clients are lifetime ones, and furthermore, although it might be a close duplication, it would never be the same product."

Back at Firmenich the perfumers return to the drawing board after receiving my comments, and in a week the modifications—or mods as they are known—arrive on my desk in Washington, D. C.

The number of bottles has multiplied. Instead of a single mod, one perfumer sends three. I started with eight, and now there are ten. Besides the anxiety of dealing with so many choices, there's also an imperiousness to being a client that discomfits me. Although I do confess to a secret, not terribly attractive, satisfaction that comes from knowing that a dismissive—too sweet!—can send the perfumers back to the drawing board.

I've told Thierry Wasser that I wish he'd made Metaphor a little less dry, and a little more floral. He responds by dumping an overload of mimosa into Mod 1. To my dismay the fragrance has changed completely. Its subtlety has been replaced by a saccharine sweetness. *It's ruined,* I lament, in my critique to Cathleen Montrose. *I mention jasmine tea and he sticks his chin in the air, runs out to the perfumer's equivilant of a florist's shop, and says, "You want floral; I'll give you floral." Sabotage!*

In response to my complaint that Mirage is too heady, Annie has toned down the wild rose and made it fresher smelling. While still lush and sophisticated, it's less obviously voluptuous. I wear it to work one day and receive several compliments. The unexpected attention causes me to reevaluate the submission. *Love at second sight. Maybe I can be Madame X after all,* I write Montrose.

Harry softens Wraparound. He adjusts the amount of vanilla (there are three different vanillas in this fragrance, each slightly different in character, he tells me), making it less sweet without sacrificing its silkiness. But I'm still not completely satisfied. *Could he, would he, nudge it one tiny step in the same direction?* I ask by return fax. Despite Cathleen Montrose's protestations that I'm not being difficult, I see myself

as the monster client. The Queen ("Off with their heads!") of Fragrance. Will I ever be satisfied? At the magazine I write for, we always say you never finish a story. You abandon it. Is it the same with perfume?

Despite my anxiety about being labeled too fussy, I'm an easy client according to the perfumers. Thierry Wasser remembers doing as many as a thousand modifications for one client. Sometimes, after working through hundreds of mods, client and perfumer end up back where they started. The client decides the original submission was the right one after all. Should the perfumer gnash his teeth silently, the client will never know. Their job is to please the client.

I also discover what everyone else in the business knows. One of the most daunting challenges in this process is language. It's the problem of explaining to the perfumer what you want. The more I can articulate my likes and dislikes, the easier it is for the perfumer to give me what I want. The worst offender is the client who says, "I know what I want when I smell it." Because words often aren't enough, clients will sometimes create a storyboard to illustrate the concept they are hoping for from the perfumers. Some do more. In the briefing process for Contradiction, Calvin Klein Cosmetics sent the competing suppliers an orchid to signal the perfumers that the perfume being developed ought to contain orchid as one of the ingredients.

Suppliers have their own motivational strategies. For a recent project involving a sports-themed Tommy Hilfiger fragrance (the brief spoke of an adrenaline rush), Quest, the supplier, sent perfumers from its New York office on a skydiving jaunt. "Much to the horror of the president of our company," reports Paul Austin, director of marketing. For a Serge Lutens fragrance, Féminité du Bois, based on a memory of the scent of a cedarwood sawmill in Morocco, perfumers from the Paris office went to that same sawmill to experience the smell for themselves. For a fragrance brief that specified a desert flower feel, another company sent its perfumers from New Jersey to California's Mojave Desert.

Speaking about fragrance can be like trying to get a toehold on a cloud. I grope for words and turn mute in the

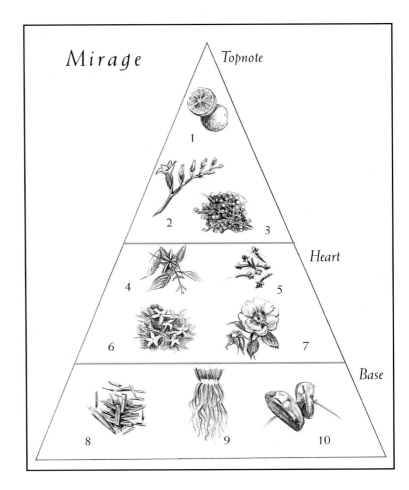

A blueprint for Mirage, a perfume commissioned by author Cathy Newman, shows the different notes, or ingredients, used by perfumer Annie Buzantian in composing the fragrance.
TOPNOTES: 1. Sicilian Bergamot; 2. Freesia; 3. Cassis Buds; HEART: 4. Night Blooming Ylang Ylang; 5. East African Clove; 6. Night Blooming Jasmine; 7. Moonlight Rose; BASE: 8. Mysore Sandlewood; 9. Vetiver; 10. Amber.

struggle to describe my wishes. There's even a term for it— the olfactory verbal gap—according to Dr. Harry Lawless, a psychologist and professor of food sciences at Cornell University. Lawless also coined the term "tip of the nose phenomenon," which is the difficulty in naming a smell in the absence of any other information. Take away the rose, he says, and 25 to 50 percent of those smelling its scent might not be able to identify it as rose.

Tongue-tied, we compensate and translate descriptions of fragrance into the language of other sensory experiences. The language of fragrance employs color, for example, using the term "a green note" to denote grass-like scents that derive from herbs and shrubs. Another means is using the imagery of music. "A top note" refers to substances that evaporate off the skin and hit the nose first, like citrus oils.

Or we rely on sheer metaphor.

One winter morning in New York I watched as eight different submissions were trotted out for Ann Gottlieb to evaluate at Firmenich. Gottlieb is a consultant, a hired nose, who has helped shepherd about a billion dollars' worth of fragrances through the creative process and on to the market. She's thin, elegant, and impeccably pulled together. The look is tailored and expensive. She wears Calvin Klein and Armani, accessorized by a Bloomingdale's shopping bag in which she totes samples of her fragrances-in-progress.

She's not a perfumer herself, but more of an interpreter and midwife to a creative process that may entail working with anyone from the Spice Girls to Christian Dior. She helps turn a thought into a scent. She can feel her way into the skin of the consumer, connecting with equal ease to the tastes of a spiky-haired teenager or a blue-haired Park Avenue matron, and create the right fragrance combination that will sell to that customer.

To please Ann Gottlieb is to please some of the heaviest hitters in the business, clients such as Calvin Klein and Elizabeth Arden. To please Ann's clients is worth millions of dollars to a supplier, which is why perfumers hang on her every word. "Never show Ann anything with cassis or honey," one perfumer told me, indicating the meticulous attention accorded her likes and dislikes. (She sails through

ABOVE A concept board created by the marketing department of International Flavors & Fragrances provides inspiration for perfumers working on fragrances for clients. BELOW The EKG-like printout of a gas chromatograph/mass spectrometer reveals a scent's chemical components.

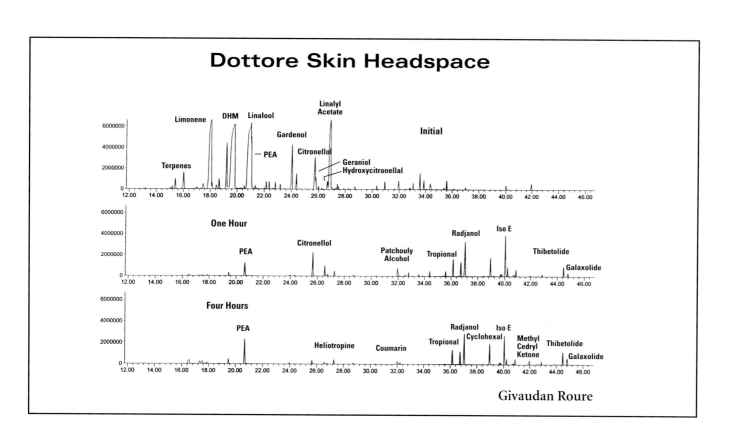

the door and her drink of choice materializes—a double decaf cappuccino with skim milk.) Gottlieb speaks for the client. If her expectations aren't met, the supplier won't win the brief. It's as easy, and as difficult, as that. She's decisive, demanding, and the master of the crisp, descriptive, sentence—an important skill in the ethereal realm of scent.

"It smells of pencil shavings," she said of a woody smelling fragrance meant for the European market. "Marshmallow cookies, the kind with coconut," she said of another, fruity, scent being offered for appraisal. "Too much like old talc. Too much 'old lady'," she said of a third.

And in the room full of perfumers everyone nodded, knowing exactly what she meant. The perfumers would return to their offices and create new submissions. Gottlieb would return in a week. The process of turning an idea into a scent would continue.

I return to Firmenich in April to evaluate round two of the modifications for the Cathy perfume. I'm beginning to get to know the perfumers, with all their strengths and vulnerabilities. Harry Frémont, a native of southern France, is the confident one. Everyone else presents two or three mods; Harry submits one. Period. It is emblematic of his passion or, perhaps, obsession, for his profession that his three daughters are named after perfumes: Lauren (a Ralph Lauren fragrance), Joy, and Estée (an Estée Lauder brand). Annie Buzantian, originally from Armenia, is the solid, supremely pragmatic, graceful one. Her neat-as-a-pin desk is every bit as composed as she is. The bright red lipstick she favors contrasts dramatically with her olive skin and dark eyes. "Other artists say they create out of misery, but I have to be happy to create," she tells me.

I do not think this is the case with Thierry Wasser. Thierry is the dark, changeable, complicated one. I never know which Thierry will greet me when I visit. Will it be the serious, formal Thierry in dark suit and tie? Or Thierry

the whimsical, in Bermuda shorts and red bow tie? At times he seems as evanescent as some of the elements he mixes. When I share my observations with Cathleen Montrose, she laughs. "Thierry is about experimentation," she says.

Experimentation. Well, isn't that the lure of fragrance, too? Who shall I be today? Shall I be the elegant, sophisticated Cathy as envisioned by Annie in Mirage? The warm, enveloping woman of Wraparound? The introspective, instinctive Zen woman of Metaphor? We reach for the object that will transform us: the wand that makes the frog a prince; the cup that brims with the elixir of love; the bottle of perfume that turns our fantasy to gold.

On the day I arrive to evaluate the second round of modifications, it's Thierry the formal. He's wearing suit and tie. He shows me Mod 2. The overdose of mimosa is gone, and Metaphor has been returned to its original formulation of orange, mint, oakmoss, tea, tobacco, and a touch of freesia.

"Okay, so I go overboard," he admits, when I reproach him about the mimosa overdose. He turns to his computer, types a few commands, and the formula for Metaphor flashes on the screen. "Look how short it is," he says, allowing me a glance. "Thirty-three ingredients. A very nice number." He looks pleased.

I make the rounds and visit the other perfumers. Annie has made Mirage even less heady and floral, and Harry has made a tiny change in Wraparound. He's reduced the vanilla ever so slightly, which tones down the sweetness even more.

It's trial and error. Like much in life, creating a perfume seems to be about stumbling along toward a solution. Each perfumer has taken a perceived aspect of me and interpreted it into a fragrance. For Harry and Wraparound, I'm the woman of two worlds: the professional writer who travels, and the mother of an adored child. In contrast, Thierry dips into the realm of the unconscious to create a fragrance

PRECEDING PAGES Model Christie Brinkley gets made up before a press event introducing her fragrance, Believe, launched by a cosmetics company. Ann Gottlieb, a leading industry consultant who helped develop the fragrance, stands in the background at right.

for the psyche—Metaphor with its yin-yang structure and irresistible name.

To watch each perfumer use me as the concept and translate my personality into a fragrance is, by turns, discomfiting and deeply moving. I see how collaborative an effort this is, how the personas of perfumer and client intermingle in the quest. It's a peculiar chemistry—of the human kind as well. When client and perfumer meet, the essential oils aren't the only volatile elements in the room.

"Women wear fragrance to be noticed," reported a Revlon survey done in the 1970s, but Cathleen Montrose demurs. Maybe then, but not now. Now women wear fragrance for themselves. They wear it to feel good. "Fragrance is an emotional cosmetic," Montrose tells me during our next meeting. She cites trend-spotter Faith Popcorn, who calls fragrance "a small indulgence."

"There's also the I.D. factor—the question of identity," Montrose says. "I don't think a fragrance can reinvent you into something you're not. But a fragrance does make you say, 'I want to buy into that image. I have a piece of Versace, or Ralph Lauren, or Calvin Klein, or whomever.' You can pick and choose. Take Calvin Klein's Eternity and its image of the perfect couple and their child. We all know that nobody has that perfect a lifestyle or marriage. After all, it's not like the old Wind Song commercials where you put on the perfume, the sky opens up, and the guy on the white horse appears. But it's still something to aspire towards."

Aspiration: the buzzword the fragrance industry loves so much. Is it wishful thinking? When we wear perfume, do we really believe it's going to make us more attractive or lovable merely because the marketing people seduce us into thinking so?

"Oh, it's not just marketing," Avery Gilbert, a sensory psychologist and industry consultant based in Montclair, New Jersey, assures me. I've called him to discuss the why-we-wear-perfume question from a psychologist's point of view. "There are many reasons people wear fragrance," he responds. "Sexual advertising is probably what drives its use. It's self-presentation, of course. But fragrance also addresses social anxieties about smelling bad—the baggage of body odor. Also, concerns about personal space: how close people allow themselves to get to one another. In Japan, you sit shoulder to shoulder. In a Mideast bazaar, you're not haggling effectively unless you're in their face. Americans are defensive. They're antsy. They have a wide perimeter. They try to get as far away as they can. Perfumes can attract, but they can also be repellent, intrusive, transgressive—the idea of the perfumed woman in the elevator invading everybody's space."

Fragrance is sold in the department store, rouged-cheek-by-powdered-jowl next to other cosmetics, but fragrance, says Ann Gottlieb, is different from lipstick, mascara, and powder. "Fragrance is more of an internal thing than makeup. It's a projection of who you are. It makes you feel good. If you pushed me, though, I might say they're both enhancers. Like control-top panty hose. It's something you know makes you look better."

Feeling good. Looking better. Fragrance—the internal, emotional cosmetic. Fragrance—a kind of lipstick for the soul. Why shouldn't romance prevail in the kingdom of possibility? We long for the dream to come true.

Winter has melted into spring. It's now early May and time is up. I'm supposed to let Cathleen know my decision. Which fragrance gets my nod as the Cathy perfume? In the real world, this is the fingernail chomping moment when the competing suppliers learn who "wins."

I need only choose among the work of five perfumers at one company. In reality, a client in the course of a project might have sampled hundreds of submissions from five or six companies. Even so, choosing a favorite is difficult. I hate making decisions. Coffee or Tea? Jamaica Blue Mountain or Mocha Kenya? Regular or Decaf? Milk or Cream? The Lady or the Tiger? To cross the Rubicon or not? I line up the finalist fragrances on my desk and spend a long time staring at them.

Finally I call Cathleen to confess I find it impossible to choose among Mirage, Metaphor, and Wraparound. No

problem, she says, why not have all three? "You can have a perfume wardrobe," she suggests. "Metaphor to write in. Mirage for an evening out. Wraparound just to feel good in." But that still means I've had to throw out the other submissions—Bois de Ile, Princess, Tempest, Savannah, and Blue Iris. Fortunately I don't have to tell the perfumers face-to-face. Cathleen will take care of that unpleasant job. But rejection hurts; I feel bad for the losers. What is it like to be a perfumer who's been told that their submission has lost? "Ask them," Cathleen says.

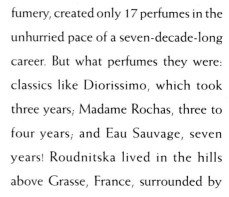

Annie assures me they learn not to take these things personally. "Well," she adds, after some thought, "you do get angry and then you mourn, but then it's time to get on to the next project." Harry says it really hurts when you see the fragrance in the store and you know it's not yours. Thierry assures me that you can be just as poor a winner as loser. Besides, he explains, rejected submissions never get wasted. They are simply reworked into another project.

"Take this mint water scent," he says. He dips a blotter into a vial and hands it to me across his desk. A sharp, green freshness envelopes me. It was, he tells me, a submission in the running for a fragrance being developed recently by an important client. "When that company dropped it, I was angry. Well, I'll use it some other time. It's a huge investment. You think I put it in the bin?"

"So when you lose," I ask him, "do you ever say, it's just a perfume?"

He frowns. "Just a perfume. Just a perfume. That's my hope, my life, myself in that bottle. It's why we're here from seven in the morning to seven at night. *Just a perfume!* When you lose a competition, you kill hope.

And when you open the bottle, a bit of us flies out."

We've completed the Cathy perfume project in eight weeks. As recently as two decades ago it might have lasted years. Edmond Roudnitska, the éminence grise of French perfumery, created only 17 perfumes in the unhurried pace of a seven-decade-long career. But what perfumes they were: classics like Diorissimo, which took three years; Madame Rochas, three to four years; and Eau Sauvage, seven years! Roudnitska lived in the hills above Grasse, France, surrounded by beautiful paintings and the flowers he adored. A man of exquisite sensibility and infinite patience, the carefully tended an orchid he'd transplanted from an Hawaiian island to his garden for years—ten years, in fact—before being rewarded with a bloom. And so it was with each perfume.

"Like the artistry of music composition or painting, the creation of the perfume may take many years. I compose what pleases me," he told NATIONAL GEOGRAPHIC writer Boyd Gibbons in 1986 in "The Intimate Sense of Smell."

In 1996, at the age of 91, Edmond Roudnitska died, and with him the luxury of time and of composing a perfume based purely on one's own convictions and taste. The Firmenich perfumers live in a different era.

Six months after beginning the Cathy perfume project, I meet Ann Gottlieb for lunch and hand her Mirage. She sprays it on her wrist, sniffs, and after a pause says, "It's right on trend. Approachable, pretty, yet doesn't scream." She looks at me quizzically. "How do you feel about it?"

"Like an imposter," I respond. "It's too pretty."

"Ah," she says, with a knowing nod. "It's aspirational."

OPPOSITE Perfume, the essence of illusion, beguiles us into believing we can be more attractive, lovable, or elegant than we may be. And yet, despite the hype and the hundreds of millions of dollars' worth of advertising that tugs at our psyche, the pleasure of an intoxicating scent is real. ABOVE The label from the author's venture into the world of fragrance creation.

Memory and Desire

Yves de Chiris has compressed 150 years of perfume history into 30 minutes. De Chiris, vice president of fine fragrance worldwide for Quest International, a supplier, is presenting his super-abridged chronicle of perfumery to an audience of more than a hundred people seated at a dozen or so round tables. It is part of a lecture series given by the Smithsonian Institution in Washington, D.C.

De Chiris is a big, vibrant man who hates ties and always wears a Nehru-collared vest, which he has hand-tailored in Pakistan. He's passionate about perfume, yet also witty with a faintly sardonic weariness. In an industry populated increasingly by executives who have cut their managerial teeth on selling fabric softeners and cereals, de Chiris (he is not reluctant to point out) is the real thing—the sixth generation son of a family of perfumers: the de Chiris of Grasse, France. He is pedigreed, with a sheen of historical association to prove it. In 1768 his family set up their first factory in Grasse to extract essential oils for perfumery. There is the portrait of his great-great-great-great-grandfather Antoine by the 18th-century French painter Jean-Honoré Fragonard; and there is the documented visit from Queen Victoria to the de Chiris factory in Grasse in 1891.

"The floor," it was noted in an account of the visit, "was spread with violets and jonquils. The royal visitors saw all the processes and examined them with interest."

The Fragonard portrait hangs on the wall of a Baltimore museum. The thank-you note from the queen's aide-de-camp hangs in de Chiris's house in Paris. The de Chiris family business was absorbed by a larger company in 1966, and the factory was subsequently sold to the town of Grasse. It was torn down and will be replaced by a public building of an as-yet unknown function. "The companies I work for get sold every ten years," de Chiris said to me with a bemused smile.

The fragrance industry has endured its share of boom and bust. From the mid-1940s until the early 1970s, "the 30 glorious years" as they were known, profits in the fragrance industry soared and pharmaceutical companies, looking to diversify, bought up suppliers as well as retail brands. Then profits turned out to be less spectacular than expected, and the sell-offs began as companies divested and went back to their core businesses. Through the flux of corporate fortunes and four different owners, de Chiris stays on, committed to fragrance and clearly reveling in his vocation.

A cloud of frankincense lifts from a clay burner in Oman. Known to the perfumer as olibanum, the fragrant resin comes from a genus of desert trees that grow wild in the Dhofar region of Oman, and in Yemen, India, Pakistan, Ethiopia, and Somalia.

De Chiris has arranged a smell-and-tell show for his lecture. In the middle of each table are dozens of tiny vials filled with perfume ingredients and well-known fragrances such as Chanel No. 5, Youth Dew, and cK One. A person designated as the "dipper" at each table will dip a handful of thin paper strips called blotters into the vials and pass them around for us to smell as the lecture progresses. "We'll focus on fragrances that have marked their decade," de Chiris promises as he projects the first slide onto the screen.

"Perfumery begins as a craft," he commences. "Fragrances were personalized creations, tailored to the client's taste." *Click!* A 17th-century engraving of a perfume seller flashes onscreen. He cites Catherine de Médicis, who created a fashion for perfumed gloves in 16th-century France. He mentions the 18th-century king, Louis XV, who had his own perfumers and distilleries, and who gave orange blossom water to all the ladies of the court at Versailles on New Year's Day.

De Chiris breezes through the 19th century, pointing out the rise of industrial, or large-scale, perfumery as opposed to the small-scale craft of the court perfumer of previous centuries. Fragrance houses like Roger et Gallet and Guerlain now bring perfumery to a broader market. He refers to perfumer François Coty, one of the first to package perfumes in crystal bottles. *Click!* A slide of Coty's 1905 perfume, Ambre Antique, appears in its Lalique bottle. The exquisite crystal bottle is an announcement to the customer that the perfume in this precious container is an item of luxury.

We are at the turn of the century. De Chiris touches on the impact of the East on European style. In fashion it manifests in a taste for turbans and Turkish cigarettes. In fragrance it is evident in a preference for woody, spicy scents such as L'Heure Bleue, created in 1912, and Mitsouko, created in 1919. (We smell L'Heure Bleue.)

"Dippers, are you keeping up with me?" De Chiris demands as he clicks away.

De Chiris plunges into the 1920s. "These were the roaring 20s," he reminds us. The constraints of previous decades are cut loose. "Women smoke, swear, and flirt. To satisfy this liberated woman, you get a new style of designer." The best of these, Coco Chanel, takes women out of their stiff corsets and puts them into comfortable, easy-to-wear clothes with clean, simple lines. Chanel's look is fresh, new, and innovative—and so is the perfume she creates. In 1921, she launches Chanel No. 5 ("Dippers! Chanel No. 5!" de Chiris prompts), and forever after the connection between fragrance and fashion becomes inseparable. *Click!* A slide of Chanel No. 5 in its black-and-white cardboard box appears on the screen. "One is struck by the simplicity and austerity of the packaging," he comments with an appreciative glance. "It is a perfect coherence of package and style."

"And in 1925," he says practically without pause, "Jacques Guerlain creates Shalimar." The fluted crystal, urn-shaped Shalimar bottle, its glass stopper as blue as a Mogul's sapphire, flashes on the screen, and from the lips of the hundred or so people present an *"ahhhh"* ripples across the room.

I am scribbling in my notebook when the *"ahhhh"* washes over me. It is so spontaneous, so unexpected, so heartfelt that I lift my head in surprise. The sound almost shimmers with longing.

Six months later that sigh still haunts me. During an interview I mention it to Jean-Paul Guerlain, grandson of Jacques Guerlain, Shalimar's creator, and wait for his reaction.

"What is left of the most beautiful lady in the world when you turn out the light?" Jean-Paul Guerlain asks in response. It is late afternoon in his Paris office, which overlooks the broad sweep of the Champs-Élysées, and the light is dimming in the room of faded gold. "You don't see her hair,

---

OPPOSITE Roman baths like these at the Maison du Bain des Nymphes at Volubilis, in Morocco, were sometimes filled with rose water. Romans wore perfume-soaked garments and shoes with scented soles. FOLLOWING PAGES Cleopatra, Queen of the Nile, luxuriated in the sensuality of fragrance, receiving the Roman statesman Mark Antony on a barge with sails soaked in perfume. Perfume served a sacred realm, too. Pharaohs burned incense to the gods.

you don't see her breasts, you don't see her jewels or the beauty of her eyes. What is left? The feminine charm of her voice and her perfume."

At last I make the connection. The slide of the bottle of Shalimar shown at the lecture evoked the sigh of remembered pleasure. It was a sigh that spoke to the lush, sensual side of perfume. Perhaps these women wore Shalimar to please a lover or husband. Perhaps it was worn by a beloved grandmother or aunt. Whatever the association, the memory was pure pleasure, an immediate, visceral response prompted by the sight of the fluted crystal bottle with its sapphire blue stopper.

Ahhhh . . .

Despite the hype, the allure of fragrance is real. The seductive power of perfume is as old as Cleopatra, who not wanting to underplay her hand, received the Roman statesman Mark Antony on a barge with sails soaked in fragrance. "So perfumed," Shakespeare tells us, "that the winds were lovesick with them."

Egyptian men and women placed perfumed unguents in their hair; the heavy oils would slowly diffuse, enrobing the wearer in an aura of scent. The elements of perfume served a more sacred realm as well: Egyptian pharaohs offered up frankincense to their gods and myrrh was used to embalm royalty. Unguent vases were among the treasures of Tutankhamen, their contents still fragrant when opened three thousand years later. The Egyptian Queen Hatshepsut sent out an argosy in search of incense and the trees that produced it. The port of Alexandria witnessed a trade in spices and aromatics. Egyptian glass and alabaster jars held perfumes mixed from frankincense out of East Africa, cedar from Lebanon, and ginger from India.

The Assyrians perfumed their beards. The Assyrian King Sardanapalus, a sybarite of the 7th century B.C., as the story goes, let it be known that the ultimate pleasure in life would be to die between his wives and his perfumes.

But the Greek philosopher Plato—who regarded the eye and ear as more noble than the nose—denounced perfumes as immoral; they were for prostitutes, he said.

Unhampered by moral rectitude, the Roman Emperor Nero bathed in rose wine. At Roman banquets, white doves with wings suffused in fragrance perfumed the air. Rose petals were showered on guests. One guest reportedly was smothered in such a deluge, thereby suffering the poetic demise of death by roses. The Romans lavished perfume on themselves, using a different scent for each part of the body. A Roman woman of social and economic standing had a small army of *ornatricis*, or slaves, in charge of the toilette. It was a life to be envied. After the bath the *tractator* would give the massage, the unctor would apply the unguents, and the *dropacistes* would care for the hands and feet. A different perfumed oil was at hand for each task. The scholar Pliny criticized such extravagance as wasteful, pointing out that perfumes gave pleasure only to others; after a while the user himself could not smell them, a factor known today as "nose fatigue."

"Take an ounce of cuttlefish powder, seven ounces of pure sandarac, four mithqals of pure aloewood . . . " begins a medieval Arabian recipe for a perfume. "The scented body is surrounded by angels," goes an Islamic saying. The writings of Arabian alchemists discussed the distillation of rose and balsam. A trade in aromatics brought incense from Yemen, musk from Tibet, sandalwood from India, and balsam from Egypt. Islamic custom dictated the sprinkling of a guest with rose water. Even today, in Saudi Arabia, a dinner party may end with the passing of the perfume: A servant splashes expensive cologne from an exquisite crystal flacon into each guest's palms; or an incense burner is set down where each woman can billow the folds of her long gown over the smoke. She will return home to her husband aromatically smoky and exotically fragrant.

By the end of the 14th century, perfume had appeared

In the home stretch, cameleers approach the ruins of Petra, in Jordan, northern terminus of the 2,400-mile-long frankincense trail. From there, spices traveled to the ports of Alexandria and Gaza for transshipment around the Mediterranean world. In Biblical times, an estimated 3,000 tons a year were exported from the Arabian peninsula.

ABOVE *An Omani tribesman chisels resin from the bark of a tree of the genus* Boswellia.
The branches bloom in September, but the harvest continues year-round.
OPPOSITE *When the branches are nicked, the resin seeps out in droplets. The first scraping is discarded.*
The second produces a gum of inferior quality. The third yields the finest quality frankincense.

in its modern incarnation—a mix of essential oils in a base of alcohol. One of the first of these, the scent known as Hungary Water, named after Queen Elizabeth of Hungary, was based on oil of rosemary and later softened by lavender oil. It was a simple formula, made up of seven or eight ingredients.

In 1573 the Earl of Oxford presented Queen Elizabeth with a pair of scented gloves, thereby shepherding into existence the fragrance industry in England. Elizabeth, captivated by fragrance, encouraged her subjects to learn how to blend and distill scented waters. Prompted by royal suggestion and example, men and women perfumed their bodies with every kind of essence from musk to lavender.

In the first half of the next century, the perfume industry in England nearly met its demise. The Reformation and its fanatic Puritanism, which culminated in the execution of Charles I in 1649, decried anything that smacked of amusement or pleasure: theater, fine clothes, and fragrance included. But with the restoration of Charles II and the monarchy in 1660, the industry rebounded. By the reign of King George III, perfume was regarded as so powerfully seductive that an act was published stating: "All women that shall seduce and betray into matrimony any of his Majesty's subjects by scents, paints, cosmetic washes . . . shall incur the penalty of the law in force against witchcraft . . . and that the marriage, upon conviction, shall stand null and void." No modern-day advertising pitch could ever come close to this endorsement of the perceived magic and power of perfume.

Across the English Channel, in 18th-century France, scented woodwork decorated the walls of many a boudoir. Men and women soaked themselves, their clothes, even their food in perfume. Versailles was *la cour parfumée*—the perfumed court. The aristocracy ordered generous amounts of perfume and often failed to pay for it. Madame Tallien, a contemporary of Marie Antoinette and a great beauty of her day, bathed each morning in crushed strawberries—more than 20 pounds of fresh berries per bath. Afterward she would be sponged gently with milk and perfume. Madame de Pompadour, it was said, spent more than one hundred thousand pounds a year on scent. Louis XIV, exquisitely sensitive to odors, had his perfumer, Monsieur Martial, create a special perfume for him every day. At the end of his life certain odors gave him a headache, but he always adored the scent of orange blossom.

In the leafy, rose-strewn gardens painted by the 18th-century French artist Jean-Honoré Fragonard, young girls in confectionary-like silk gowns seem to breathe perfume—no doubt, an essence of rose and violets—from every soft curve and crease. Similarly, in an earlier century, the Italian Renaissance painter Titian's fleshy nudes seem enveloped in the dark, golden glow of sandalwood and myrrh. "The winged genius of seduction," Patrick Grainville calls perfume in *Les Flacons de la Séduction*. "Perfume is a bewitching intruder . . . our most intimate link with others."

Perfume is bewitching, sometimes malevolently so. In the macabre novel *Perfume* by Patrick Süskind, the repugnant, but brilliant perfumer Jean-Baptiste Grenouille feverishly dedicates his life to extracting the most utterly irresistible fragrance of all: the scent of a ripe, young virgin. The English novelist Somerset Maugham, baffled by the ability of the fat and homely H. G. Wells to attract women, once asked one of Wells's mistresses what she found so attractive about him. His body smelt of honey, she replied. Historian Alain Corbin reports that Henry III, King of France, entered a room where Marie de Cleves had been changing, smelled the lingering scent of her nightgown, and remained enthralled with her for the rest of his life. Wrote Flaubert of a pair of slippers belonging to a woman he adored: "I breathe their perfume, they smell of verbena— and of you in a way that makes my heart swell."

Sex and scent are intimately linked. "I return in three days; don't bathe," Napoleon reportedly wrote Josephine while on one of his campaigns. Others prefer less earthly odors. "My wife was wearing Yves St. Laurent's Paris when we met," a man tells me, practically sighing at the memory. On a trip to Morocco I meet a vendor in the Marrakech souk who promises to sell me a perfume that will "make men fall into your arms. Will you buy?"

April is the cruelest month, T. S. Eliot wrote, breeding lilacs out of dead ground, "mixing memory and desire." Surely memory and desire are the keynotes of perfume, as we respond to fragrance viscerally, deeply, and immediately. My friend Sisse remembers the amber necklace she inherited from her mother. The beads still held the faint golden glow of Shalimar, and when she cradled them in her hands the aroma of her mother's perfume brought her to tears. Perfume has no boundaries in space or time. This, in part, is its magic.

Perfume connects with our most basic and primitive window on the world: our sense of smell. Animals use odors to perceive danger, to select food, and to mate, and to an extent so do we. We smell smoke from a fire and think danger. We smell rotten food and know to avoid it. Natural body chemicals known as pheromones and hormones play off each other in a complicated chemical Morse code signaling recognition and arousal. Much remains unknown, but recently, in work done at the Ludwig Boltzmann Institute for Urban Ethology in Vienna, Dr. Astrid Jütte demonstrated a direct link between scent and sex by exposing male nostrils to a synthetic mixture of the fatty acids found in vaginal secretions. The result: The sexual judgment of men who inhale the mixture goes askew. In the experiment the men were shown photographs of women and asked to rate them. Because of the chemical mix, women not typically considered attractive suddenly became more desirable. Perhaps the ultimate fragrance may have more to do with pheromones and hormones than jasmine and rose.

What else might work its olfactory magic on men? In a 1995 study Dr. Alan Hirsch, a neurologist and psychiatrist at the Smell and Taste Treatment and Research Foundation in Chicago, found that the smell of pumpkin pie had a greater effect on male sexual arousal than any other scent tested. Hirsch's researchers used tiny cuffs to measure penile blood flow as an indicator of arousal. The winning fragrance was a mixture of lavender and pumpkin pie, resulting in a 40 percent increase in blood flow. The scent of roses prompted a mere 3.5 percent increase in flow.

Hirsch's findings, known in the industry as the pumpkin pie study, provoked its share of skepticism. "A weird study," a scientist in the field commented to me. In fairness, Hirsch seems somewhat baffled by the results himself. "We didn't know what it meant," he admits, "other than medical students are always hungry . . . or maybe it's that men are inherently very arousable anyway."

Should the fragrance industry toss out Obsession and Opium and work instead on an eau de pumpkin pie?

"I suppose if the aim of a perfume is to induce male sexual arousal, you're better off using a food item than any of the perfumes we tested," Hirsch says, noncommittally. Meanwhile, the industry-supported Olfactory Research Fund has announced that it will fund its own study of the relationship between scent and sensuality. Its investigators are Drs. Cynthia Graham, Erick Janssen, and Stephanie Sanders of Indiana University; the latter two hail from the mecca of sex research, the Kinsey Institute for Research

A wealth of spices spills from a vendor's display in a Yemeni market.
In the ancient world, spices and resins were emblematic of the rare and costly. Frankincense and
myrrh—among the most precious commodities of that time—were among offerings carried by the Magi.

in Sex, Gender, and Reproduction. "Women," writes Dr. Graham, "will be asked to wear scented 'necklaces' as they observe a sexually erotic film, a sexually neutral film, or fantasize." The study, the Olfactory Research Fund says, will address "what we all want to know: the effect of a commercially successful perfume on . . . sensual and erotic experience."

Odors bond mothers and their infants. To a mother, there is no fragrance more intoxi-cating than the smell of her new-born's head. "It smells like caramel, it smells so sweet, so wonder-ful . . . once you've smelled them there, you love them whether they're your own or somebody else's," effuses the wet nurse in Patrick Süskind's novel *Perfume*.

We don't yet know if infants can smell in the womb, but the sensory equipment is in place from the second trimester on. Animal research has shown that odors and flavors in utero can affect diet preferences later in life. Sometimes scent can be a matter of life and death. A mother rat licks her nipples so her blind pups can follow the scent of her saliva to milk. Wash the nipples and the pups lose their way. Experiments in humans have shown that by the age of six weeks, nursing infants can distinguish their mothers by smell.

The scents of our childhood linger half-buried in memory, awaiting the faintest cue to re-emerge. In New York a perfumer tells me of a submission for a client inspired by a childhood memory of putting his face in his mother's handbag and inhaling the comingled scents of lipstick, powder, and leather. The French designer Jean-Paul Gaultier has created a perfume bearing his name based

on his memory of the face powder his grandmother wore.

Sometimes fragrance taps into the well of memory and desire with deliberate vengeance. Joséphine, when dumped by Napoleon in favor of Marie-Louise, daughter of the Emperor of Austria, saturated the rooms of the royal apartment in musk, which her former husband hated. So, too, I heard a modern-day version of that story about a jilted girlfriend, who before her furious departure, poured an entire bottle of her perfume on her ex's sheets—a memento for him to remember her by.

Memory and fragrance are inter-twined, some biologists insist, because the sense of smell plugs directly into the limbic system, the seat of emotion and memory in the brain. Unlike sight and sound, which are dependent on impulses of energy, smell is a chemical sense. A scent is made up of chemical mol-ecules. Sniff a rose and molecules of its fragrance rush through your nostrils where they are warmed, humidified, and then channeled up two narrow chambers until, finally, they wind up at the olfactory epithelium, located at the roof of each nasal cav-ity just beneath the brain. The olfactory epithelium, a pair of dime-sized mucous-covered patches, is made up of mil-lions of tall, slim cells packed together. Some of them, the olfactory sensory cells, have tiny hair-like cilia with recep-tor sites that capture and bind the molecules.

How the molecules get translated by the receptors into a smell is still a matter of conjecture. In one scenario, the stereo-chemical theory of odor, the mechanism is a lock and key arrangement in which a molecule of scent fits into a receptor and switches it on. In another, more recent line of thought known as the vibrational theory of

ABOVE To begin with, perfume bottles were made of simple materials, like the first century A.D. animal-shaped container from ancient Greece made of terra cotta. OPPOSITE A cherished fragrance was once stored in this sixth century A.C. Egyptian vessel made of wood.

odor, some scientists speculate that molecules vibrate and switch on the receptor. It's like hitting the right pitch on a tuning fork and having a door, attuned to that particular pitch, open in response.

Either way, when a fragrance molecule interacts with a receptor it fires a signal to the olfactory bulbs of the brain. From there it's a straight shot via the limbic system to the cortex and to the realization that "That's a rose!" and then to the swiftly summoned memory—"A rose! That reminds me of the crystal vase of red roses that stood on the grand piano in my grandmother's living room. She always smelled of lavender and face powder. How much I miss her."

No other sense has such immediate access to the brain and to our own personal museum of memory. It is a matter of seconds from whiff to unreeling memory, says Dr. David Rubin, a psychologist at Duke University. "Proust got it right," he says. He means the scene in *Remembrance of Things Past*, where the taste and scent of a madeleine, a small cake, dipped in tea takes the narrator back to his childhood village of Combray. Says Dr. Rubin, "It took Proust two pages to get there. It takes us 15 seconds."

The scent of Johnson & Johnson baby powder, Play-Doh, and the antiseptic-plastic smell of Band-Aids are the madeleines for those of us who grew up in the fifties and sixties—a fact well-noted by trend-spotters in the fragrance industry. In studies, odors bearing the scent of Johnson & Johnson baby powder, the product most immediately associated with infant care in the United States, has been found to have a soothing effect. But only in this country.

Such information is a gold mine for trend hunters as they look for the Next Big Thing. What's next? Possibly, I am told, the scent of a computer keyboard. Can chocolate-computer chip fragrance be far behind?

Thanks to the fast-forward nature of the fragrance industry, I probably won't have to wait long. A press release crosses my desk, announcing that a new brand of perfume called Smell THIS is making its market debut. The release touts a line of fragrances about "real smells and real people," a "true lifestyle fragrance concept that

disposes of the artificial dreams of traditional perfumes, while focusing in on genuineness and individuality." Among the offerings: such "techno-pop, retro-fume" scents as Cake Batter, Leather Jacket, Fluffy Pillow, and Head Shop. Soon-to-come fragrances in the new line—the Haz Mat series, featuring scents such as Gasoline, Car Wax, Bug Spray, and Smoke.

I prefer my nostalgia in a more gentle guise. My mother wore Guerlain's L'Heure Bleue. To unstopper that dusky scent returns me to my child-self, tucked into bed; late at night, after being out to dinner, my mother would come into my room to kiss me, enveloping me in a cloud of powdery warmth. A friend remembers the bottle of Joy, the liquid itself yellow as a canary diamond ("the costliest perfume in the world," the ads claimed), that stood on her mother's dressing table. But that was her "trophy" bottle, my friend explains. The perfume her mother actually wore was Youth Dew—the liquid in the bottle dark as maple syrup; its scent, thick and dark as well.

Anything with gardenia reminds me of Miami Beach, where I grew up, and of nights fragrant with the warmth of tropical blooms. The oystery smell of the sea also summons Miami, which is perhaps why I went through a phase of adoring L'Eau d'Issey, with its marine-like astringency. The sea smell, I am told, comes from a fragrance chemical called calone. Of course it is not calone I think of when I wear it, but rather my own seashore memories of sand and salt air.

For Thierry Wasser, one of the perfumers at Firmenich in New York, the scent of Chanel's Cuir de Russie conjures memories of his father. One morning I sat in Wasser's office high above the urban frenzy of Madison Avenue as he dipped blotters into vials. He was showing me several of his works in progress when the conversation shifted unexpectedly and he began to talk about the power of scent to crack open the heart.

"My father always wore driving gloves," Wasser said as he pushed aside the small vials and began to toy with a bottle of cologne in front of him. "He would splash on his fragrance, pull on his gloves, and drive off. He left for good when I was three. He died when I was 15. He pulled off the road in the south of France and slumped over the wheel. A heart attack.

"At 18 I learned to drive. I took out his gloves, and when I put them on the warmth of my hands released the scent of cologne."

Wasser and I stared at each other in silence for a moment. Then he dipped a blotter into the bottle of Cuir de Russie on his desk and waved it under my nose.

"The ghost in the bottle," he said.

Fragrance creates a legacy. Perfumes skip a generation says Geoffrey Webster, of Givaudan Roure. He maintains that you wear the perfume your grandmother wore, not what your mother wore. Perhaps the generational skip is for psychoanalysts to ponder; after all, the relationship with one's grandmother is easier, less contentious, than the mother/daughter connection. I mention the theory of generational skipping to my friend Kathy, adding: "But of course this doesn't apply to you, since I know you don't wear perfume."

"On the contrary," she replies. "My grandmother always smelled of traditional formula Jergens hand lotion. It's the only scent she ever wore. It's the only scent I wear, too."

L'Air du Temps by Nina Ricci reminds me of my ninth-grade English teacher, a tall, angular, model-thin woman, who would stride down the hall leaving a wake of perfume behind her. Such a fragrance wake is known as *sillage*—a scent trail, of sorts. To the chemist, sillage is part of a carefully considered factor known as diffusivity, how a fragrance diffuses or spreads. The other factor, substantivity, how long a fragrance lingers on skin, varies from person to person according to ethnic and racial background, skin type, and sheer individual chemistry.

"Think of yourself as a steam radiator," explains Ken Purzycki, director of fragrance science at Givaudan Roure. "When you wear perfume, it evaporates. The rate of evaporation varies, even from arm to arm. The right arm, if you happen to be right-handed, will evaporate more quickly, since the increased muscle mass translates into a slightly higher temperature—as much as one to two degrees. In fact, I can tell whether a person is left- or right-handed most of the time by measuring the temperature of each hand." Oilier skins hold fragrance better than drier skins do. It's a delicate chemistry. Chanel No. 19 may smell wonderful on me, horrible on you. Perfume needs the warmth of skin to show it off. Never buy fragrance without trying it on.

"The thing about perfume is that you are the arbiter," says Annette Green, president of the Fragrance Foundation, an industry-funded educational organization that promotes the use of scent. "There's a real personal relationship between self and product. Which is why you hear women say sometimes: Such and such doesn't smell good on my skin." For a perfume to work, you must, as the French say, *être bien dans sa peau*—feel good in one's own skin.

And so, perfume is skin-deep—and deeper. Perfume is about beauty—it can make us feel good. Perfume is about memory—it can make us feel confused. A man confesses to me that for him Chanel No. 5 is dangerous and problematic. As a child of ten or eleven, he and his mother were on a speedboat that caught fire; for an afternoon the two were stranded on an island. "I fell asleep next to her," he said, recalling the smell of hot sand and sea and the rich, lush scent of his mother's Chanel No. 5. "It's in my mind forever." Our personal archive of scent reaches into the darkest corners of mind and heart.

In the Paris suburb of Versailles I visit a scent archive of a less personal nature, a museum of perfumes called the Osmothèque. It is a library of fragrant smells, housed in a contemporary concrete and glass building next to a 19th-century stone mansion that houses the *Institut Supérieur International du Parfum, de la Cosmétique, et de l'Aromatique Alimentaire* (ISIPCA), a school where perfumers are trained. How fitting that the building which houses the historical past of perfume should stand side-by-side with its future.

One raw, wet day in spring, I found myself walking down a short flight of concrete steps behind curator André Gerber to the very heart of the Osmothèque, a basement

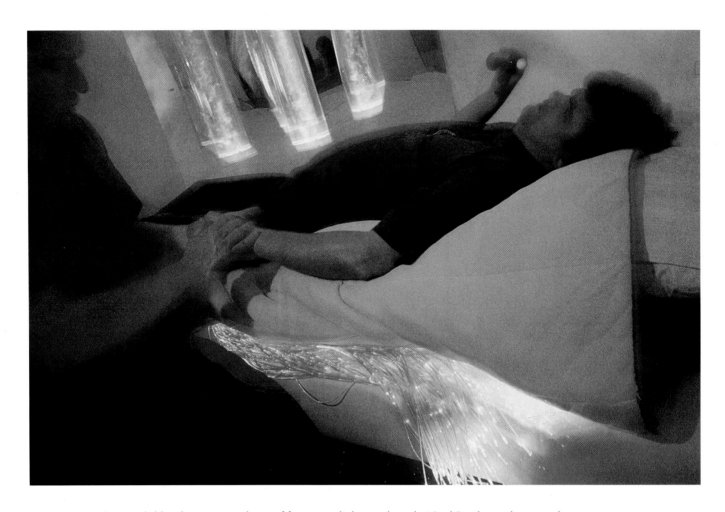

Surrounded by the sensory embrace of fragrance, lights, and touch, Nigel Brailey undergoes a therapy session at Andlaw House, a therapeutic residence in Exeter, England. The facility has pioneered the use of scent in helping the impaired. New research indicates that smells may be able to influence our minds, moods, and bodies.

room archive of fragrances from around the world. The room is ringed by floor-to-ceiling steel shelves holding more than 1,100 fragrances, some extremely old and rare. The room itself is a study in contrast. The cold steel shelving and stone walls belie the warmth and softness of the perfume, which is contained in metal flasks about the size of large coffee thermoses. The 95 companies whose fragrances form the core of the collection commit to giving the Osmothèque 500 grams (17.6 ounces) of every new perfume they create. "The Osmothèque is a safety deposit box for fragrance," Gerber explained.

Alongside the new perfumes are more than 250 scents that have completely disappeared from the world: obscure perfumes with strange names like Lasso and Wilted Carnation. Ten of these perfumes are by Paul Poiret, the first couturier to create a perfume. They exist because a perfumer named Youri M. Gutsatz thought to record the formulas in a notebook when the company he worked for bought Rosine, the company that manufactured the Poiret perfumes decades ago. Other formulas came from company records or old books and documents pertaining to perfumery. Why do perfumes disappear? It is like fashion; a perfume can go out of style. It can become too expensive to produce, the company that produced it fails to support it, or the company itself goes out of business.

The safety deposit box, as Gerber calls his fragrance archive, is chilly. The room is kept in darkness at a constant 54°F, since light and heat are two great enemies of perfume. (This is why, if you don't mind the

Playing a game of exquisite subtlety, practitioners of the ancient Japanese art of kodo try to identify different fragrances.
The Japanese use fragrance in the bath, home, and office, but perfume itself has traditionally been a gift to be admired,
not used. The impact of Western culture on Japan is changing that as a younger generation moves into place.

inconvenience, your refrigerator is the best place to store perfume.) "Oxygen is the third enemy of fragrance," explains Gerber, "and so we top off the bottles with argon gas, which is inert. When we want to sample a fragrance, we siphon off about a sixth of an ounce into a small vial."

So that I might smell some of these rare fragrances for myself, Gerber had done just that. The vials, several dozen or so, were neatly arranged on a table in an amphitheater-like classroom. One by one, we sampled the smells of centuries past. It was a waltz through time and decades often more gracious than our own. "I will show you the oldest one first," he announced to us as he dipped a blotter into the 14th-century scent Eau de La Reine de Hongrie, also called Hungary Water,

which smelled medicinal, like an herbal cough drop. The formula, found in old manuscripts and re-created by the Osmothèque, is made from plants like rosemary, sage, and citrus. "A woman of a certain age with aches was advised to rub herself with this cologne and to put a few drops in her consommé," Gerber related. "She did, and she felt so young that the King of Poland asked her to marry him even though he was 30 years younger."

"Here is Arlequinade," Gerber said, holding up another

vial. "It's a Paul Poiret fragrance from 1910. We are not sure exactly which was his first, perhaps Pierrot in 1905. In all, he created 36 perfumes." He proudly dipped a blotter into Arlequinade and offered it for evaluation. It smelled slightly musty, grandmotherly even, with a hint of moss and the heaviness of roses.

"About eight years ago a tiny woman, bent with age, came to see us," Gerber said "'I want to find my mother,' the woman said." Gerber was puzzled until she explained that it was her mother's fragrance she was searching for. She wanted to smell Arlequinade. "It hadn't been made in years until we remade it for our collection," he told me, as I breathed in its mossy, floral scent. "We allowed her to smell it. And she walked away happy."

There was Un Air Embaumé from 1919, with its soft, amber glow, and Joy, created by the French couturier Jean Patou in 1930. There was also the bold, sharp green scent of Vent Vert, created in 1945 by one of the first woman perfumers, Germaine Cellier. And there was the 1947 Jacques Fath perfume, Iris Gris, as luminescent as moonlight with its soft, silvery base of Tuscan iris. Joy and Vent Vert are still sold, but not Iris Gris. "It is too expensive to produce today," Gerber said, his voice tinged with sadness.

And now, Gerber announced, I would smell

Eau de Cologne de Napoléon I à Sainte-Hélène: The cologne that Napoleon wore during his years of exile on the tiny island of St. Helena, 1,200 miles off the coast of Africa.

Napoleon adored cologne; he used it obsessively. A flask of eau de cologne tucked into his boot accompanied him on campaigns and sweetened the stench of war. On the battlefield he drenched himself in cologne, using a bottle, sometimes two, each day. At court, as emperor, a bottle of the finest scent was poured over his head and shoulders each morning. He placed an order for toiletries shortly before his defeat at Waterloo.

"I feel the infinite in myself," said Napoleon. As the man who held the reins of power over most of Europe for a decade, he must have felt it was so. Hadn't he successfully conquered the powerful realms of Austria, Italy, and Russia? Later, in exile on St. Helena, in the middle of the South Atlantic Ocean, his weary bones felt nothing but the finiteness of mortality. For five and a half years, until his death in 1821, Napoleon, the self-crowned Emperor of France, the commander who had led two million French soldiers into 60 battles, was imprisoned in a shack.

He had a valet, Ali the Mameluke, who was directed to write to Fargeon, one of Napoleon's perfumers. Would the perfumery kindly send the formula for Napoleon's cologne? It did, and so the dutiful Ali gathered what ingredients he could on St. Helena and compounded Napoleon's fragrance.

Some years ago Ali's personal belongings were put up for auction. The former Mayor of Versailles bought a chest of drawers at the sale, discovered the formula in a drawer, and brought it to the Osmothéque. Jean Kerleo, past president of the French Society of Perfumers and a director of the Osmothéque, was given the formula and asked to remake it. It was not an easy task, Kerleo explained to me when I interviewed him. It was impossible to get the exact ingredients Ali had used, but finally, after a month of trial and error, he held in his hand a re-creation of the cologne Napoleon had worn in exile. "It was a very moving moment," Kerleo said simply.

Finally, Gerber dipped a blotter into a small vial and handed it to me to smell. The cologne was crisp and lemony, as fresh and sweet as a summer day—the very opposite of a dark, smoky battlefield with its stench of blood and gunpowder.

What must it have been like for Napoleon, the prisoner, to splash on the same scent he wore as Napoleon, the conqueror of Europe?

"It evoked his heroic period. Of course it made him happy to have his cologne," said Gerber.

The ghost in the bottle.

We forget. Time passes. Faces fade. Events grow dim. Then the whiff of something—a touch of citrus, perhaps—crosses our path. And we remember.

Captivated by fragrance, Napoleon, here portrayed by the French artist Jacques-Louis David, poured a bottle or two of eau de cologne over his body each day. Scent masked the stench of war. He placed an order for toiletries shortly before his defeat at Waterloo in 1815.

THREE

The Art of the Perfumer

To make a perfume, take four or five or hundreds of ingredients, known in the industry as notes, and add one perfumer.

First of all, what is a note? In short, it's a word borrowed from music to indicate the characteristic odor of a single material. The world of perfumery allows for more than 2,000 notes to choose from, but many are simply variations on a theme, such as rose notes. There are light, sparkling, citrus notes like lemon or grapefruit. Dark, resiny notes like balsam or olibanum, also known as frankincense. Fragrant, woody notes like sandalwood or cedar. Bracing, herbal notes like lavender or basil.

Some notes are utterly noxious. Cassis, or black currant, smells like cat urine. Animal notes such as civet, from the gland of a small wildcat native to North Africa, and castoreum, the glandular secretions from a beaver, are unmistakably fecal. Used sparingly, in just the right amount, they anchor a fragrance, giving it roundness and longevity. Aldehyde, the synthetic chemical that gives Chanel No. 5 its sparkle, smells like starched laundry. And orris, which comes from the rhizome of an iris and is the most expensive

natural material of all at $40,000 a pound, smells like burnt candle wax.

There are approximately 20 rose notes to consider. Do you want Bulgarian, Moroccan, Turkish, or French rose? A blend? A synthetic substitute like rhodinal, perhaps? "Choosing a note is like picking a color, say blue, then picking a shade in that color," says Steve De Mercado, a perfumer with Givaudan Roure, one of the leading fragrance suppliers.

The perfumer acts as composer. The arrangement of a perfume is not unlike a three-part fugue. The part of a perfume known as the top, or head note, spins off the skin immediately; it's a fanfare and vanishes in minutes. The middle note, or heart—compounded of heavier materials that last for hours—helps set the theme of the fragrance. The bottom note, or dry down, gives depth and, like a resonating chord, can persist for a day or two.

It's all part of the orderly chemical process called evaporation. Lighter molecules, like citrus and fruity notes, evaporate quickly; they reach the nose first. Heavier molecules,

A rare luxury edition flacon for the Roger & Gallet perfume Peau d'Espagne was created by the French glass artisan, Daillet. Such artists took the perfume bottle from a simple container and raised it to the level of sculptural art.

like resins and woods, evaporate more slowly; they reach the nose later. The rate at which different materials evaporate is only one of many things a perfumer must learn.

"Creation of perfume starts from knowledge," Jean Kerleo says. "Knowledge of raw materials. Knowing how they evolve. How they change."

Kerleo, a courtly, gray-haired man, is chief perfumer for Jean Patou, a fragrance house. Joy is their most famous perfume. Today, nearly every perfumer in the business works for one of the big suppliers. Kerleo is one of the few exceptions. If the house of Jean Patou decides to launch a new fragrance, it will not be put out for bid with the suppliers. Kerleo will create it in-house. He is an elder statesman of the craft, understated, polite, and discreet, with an archive of knowledge bestowed by 44 years' experience as a perfumer. In another era he might be an adviser at court, quietly murmuring counsel in the king's ear.

I am sitting in his office, in the Paris suburb of Saint-Ouen, when he reaches behind his desk and shows me a twisted white tuber about the length of my index finger.

"It is orris, the source of the scent of iris," he explains. The root, which grows in Italy, must soak in water for two years before being dried, ground, and made into orris butter. It is the soft, luminous base for such perfumes as Chanel No. 19 and Guerlain's L'Heure Bleue.

Putting the orris down, he lifts a small tin from a shelf and opens it to show me a fist-sized lump, as dense and brown as a small potato. It's ambergris, another costly raw material (replaced today by synthetic substitutes like ambroxan and amberlyn). Ambergris is formed by whales when they feed on cuttlefish and are unable to digest the beaks. They regurgitate the greasy mass, which floats and eventually beaches on a shore. It's a fixitive, a stabilizer, that burnishes the glow of other ingredients, imparts a velvety

feel to a fragrance, and allows it to linger on the skin. It is heavenly when aged and dissolved in a tincture of alcohol. When fresh, it is nauseating, greasy, and repugnant in appearance. "So many ingredients are so ugly," Kerleo marvels, replacing the lid. "Who could imagine they could smell so glorious?"

The art of perfumery is an enchantment. An ugly, white root becomes the soft, silvery base of Chanel No. 19. The undigested remains of a dyspeptic whale's lunch enhances the golden glow of Shalimar. Magic: The ugly duckling becomes a swan.

"I have a story for you," Kerleo says. "Ten years ago I organized a conference about Ernest Beaux, the creator of Chanel No. 5. There was an old perfumer there who had known Beaux. He talked about the day a journalist came to see Ernest Beaux, and told him, 'To me, you are the greatest perfumer in the world.'

"'I am honored by the compliment,' Beaux replied. 'But, you know, when I use vanilla, I make crème caramel, whereas Jacques Guerlain creates a Shalimar.'"

I have seldom heard a more generous comment. After all, I tell Kerleo, Beaux was certainly no slouch as a perfumer.

"It's not that Beaux was any less a perfumer than Guerlain," Kerleo responds. "It's a matter of style. Guerlain was a genius at soft, ambery, sweet perfumes like Shalimar. But he may not have been able to produce a Chanel No. 5."

But even the greatest perfumers can fail. Who, besides a historian, remembers Sous le Vent, created by Jacques Guerlain eight years after Shalimar?

"Nothing is certain," Kerleo says. "Sometimes you know you have done a perfume that is very, very good and it doesn't sell. Have you smelled Iris Gris?"

I remembered it well. It was one of the old perfumes André Gerber had allowed me to sample at the Osmothèque a few days earlier. I recalled its soft, powdery

CLOCKWISE FROM TOP A palette of herbs and spices inspire perfumers who rely on such ingredients to create a fragrance: orange peel, sweet basil, English lavender, Dainty Bess rosebuds, lemon verbena, larkspur, bayberry, vetiver root, assorted rosebuds, coriander, sage, bay leaves, and juniper. At the center is an artistic combination of the surrounding ingredients.

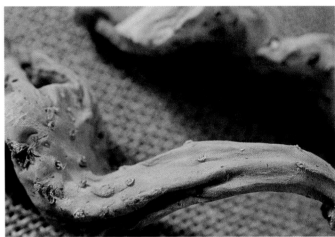

CLOCKWISE FROM TOP LEFT *Among the thousands of notes in the perfumer's repertoire: nutmeg, a spicy note; orris root, or iris, a soft, silvery, floral note infused into "orris butter," which sells for $40,000 a pound; tonka bean, a vanilla substitute; and olibanum, a resin also known to the perfumer as frankincense.*

CLOCKWISE FROM TOP LEFT *Among the thousands of notes in the perfumer's repertoire: nutmeg, a spicy note; orris root, or iris, a soft, silvery, floral note infused into "orris butter," which sells for $40,000 a pound; tonka bean, a vanilla substitute; and olibanum, a resin also known to the perfumer as frankincense.*

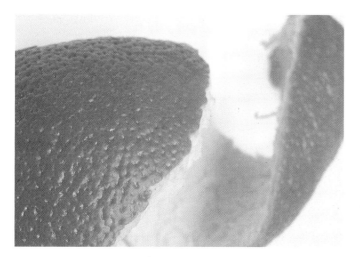

CLOCKWISE FROM TOP LEFT *The geography of perfume includes such natural ingredients as: orange peel from California and Florida; lavender from England and France; oakmoss from Yugoslavia and Morocco; musk from China. The latter has been replaced by synthetic substitutes.* FOLLOWING PAGES *Jasmine, here being harvested in India, is also grown for perfumery in Egypt and Morocco.*

ABOVE *Sophia Grosjman, a star in the universe of perfumery and creator of dozens of well-known fragrances, samples a work in progress in the laboratory at IFF headquarters in New York.* FOLLOWING PAGES *Perfumers Rodrigo Flores-Roux and Alienor D'Aumale sniff a fragrance as it lifts from the skin of a test subject at IFF. The evaluation of a fragrance as it reacts with skin and evaporates is a critical part of the developmental process.*

ABOVE *Sophia Grosjman, a star in the universe of perfumery and creator of dozens of well-known fragrances, samples a work in progress in the laboratory at IFF headquarters in New York.* FOLLOWING PAGES *Perfumers Rodrigo Flores-Roux and Alienor D'Aumale sniff a fragrance as it lifts from the skin of a test subject at IFF. The evaluation of a fragrance as it reacts with skin and evaporates is a critical part of the developmental process.*

fragrance. It seemed as richly elegant as a gown made of heavy silver satin. I adored it.

"It's wonderful." He nodded. "Very expensive to make. It should have worked, but it never had any success. Instead, it disappeared. It's always after the fact that you explain success and failure. Sometimes you miss being in style. You're too late. Or you're too early. Or there's a miss somewhere and the name doesn't fit the bottle. Or the bottle doesn't fit the name. Sometimes it's the marketing. For some reason you're not reaching the right group of consumers." A shadow of sadness passed over his face.

"What's given you the most pleasure in what you do?" I asked, hoping to steer him to a more cheerful subject.

He brightened. "The creation, clearly. And the fact of being able to touch and select my raw materials. To control the perfume from A to Z. It's not in my office that I create my perfumes. It's the odd moment here or there. When I can't sleep at night. Even in my car, coming to work. You are listening to music, you think of work, and you think: "What if . . .

"Imagination. Fantasy. It's the difference between a chemist and a perfumer. You dream your perfume before you write the formula. It's not just chance. It's not just exact science. There will always be things that won't work. You begin your fragrance as a composer, putting elements together. You finish your fragrance as a sculptor, shaping and paring them down."

"And you have to be crazy in a way," adds Sophia Grojsman, of IFF.

If Jean Kerleo embodies courtly Old World refinement and understatement, Sophia Grojsman is his flamboyant New World opposite. As Kerleo might say, it's a question of style.

On the day I visit her in New York at IFF, a building with a waffle-like facade on 57th Street, Grojsman wears a black leather skirt bisected by a huge metal zipper, a leopard print blouse, tottery black high heels, and black stockings. She has a broad, generous mouth, coated in crimson lipstick, heavily lined brown eyes, and she speaks Russian-accented English—the remnant of a childhood spent in Belarus (the land between Poland and Russia annexed by the former Soviet Union after World War I).

As a child Grojsman played with flowers. "I was born after the war and there weren't many toys," she says. She is still playing with flowers, only now they bloom in the bottle. As IFF's star perfumer Grojsman has worked on blockbuster fragrances like Eternity, Trésor, and Paris.

Grojsman works at a half-moon-shaped fruitwood desk, its surface all but obliterated by rows of bottles. "I started here as a laboratory technician 30 years ago," she tells me. "I trained as an analytic chemist in Poland. But originally they didn't want to hire me. They said I was overqualified. Well, I needed the job and they hired me anyway.

"Every free minute I had after compounding for the perfumer I would sneak off and experiment on my own. I would look at a formula and realize it could be simplified. I could take a whole page formula and boil it down. So I made a base minus those ingredients. When she needed me to redo it, rather than waste a half a day, I could compound it in a fraction of the time. The perfumer thought I was so fast. I was afraid she would find out. I never told."

Says a rival perfumer, "It's like squeezing a fruit. Sophia takes a formula and just by looking at it gets to its essence. It's a true gift and it's inventive."

An assistant in a lab coat walks in. "He wants wild meadow numbers 4, 5, and 6," she says to Grojsman. Translation: Someone, perhaps an evaluator acting as liaison between client and perfumer, wants to see three new versions of a scent in progress. *Right now.*

"I don't believe it," Grojsman says, hand on forehead. "Insanity. When people have to create something that doesn't exist, that person has to have the freedom to think."

She leans forward conspiratorially. "I am going to close the door and do something illegal. I am going to light a cigarette."

"But doesn't the smoke affect . . . ?" I ask.

"I bypass it," she says brushing off the question as if it

were a stray ash. "I go right to the heart of a fragrance. Some people smell top notes first. I go deeper. I search for the *soul*.

"I don't like the idea that I'm called a nose," she says dismissively. "Everyone is a nose. It's creativity and passion that makes a perfumer. I can dream perfumes. I can smell them in my head. I can feel them."

The assistant scurries in with two blotters. Grojsman waves one, then the other, briefly beneath her nose. There is a pause, then a nod of approval. "I like the new one better." The assistant looks relieved.

"My work comes home with me," Grojsman continues. "I live with these fragrances days, months. I put them on in the middle of the night. My husband will say: Can I smell? But the public is what I count on. Taxi drivers are the best. Once I was working on something very sexy, very spiritual; I got into a cab wearing it, and there is an Indian guy. He's saying, 'I can't drive. I can't drive.' He loved it. He was ready to give me a longer ride.

"And once, when I was finishing work on the Yves Saint Laurent perfume Paris, I put it on to test it and walked out. It was about 9:30 at night. A man—he was drunk—started following me. I started running. He continued to follow. And I'm running and he's running, and then he says, 'Please don't run. I like this perfume!'" She smiles broadly.

"The proudest moment for me is to know I am making some woman happy. Or maybe someone suddenly turned his nose, liked what he smelled, and got attracted to the person."

"Did you ever work on a man's fragrance?" I ask.

"Once. But the project was canceled. It's not necessarily my thing. But if I ever do make one, it will be from a female perspective. A man's fragrance as dreamed by a woman."

"Is there a signature to your work?" I wonder.

"I am known as the Queen of Roses. A rose is a flower of love. You don't see a man bringing a woman a dozen orange blossoms. I don't care how many fragrances are made. There is no such thing as not having a rose.

"There has to be soul, too. There has to be personality." And there is—Grojsman's perfumes overflow with personality; they are great, big, gorgeous creations that radiate sensuality.

"There was once a bottom note I thought was sexy," she recalls. "I called it 'topless'. Someone here in the lab didn't understand." Grojsman sniffed.

"'What does this mean?' this person, who was almost a nun, asked as she pointed to the formula.

"'Topless means without a top!' I told her.

"The old perfumers like François Coty probably made one or two trial compounds a day. They completed the fragrance in three or four years. Those were the real creators in my opinion. These days we might have three weeks to come up with a new fragrance. And I turn around and say, 'Really? Three weeks?' You know you are fooling yourself. You can't. You can't. Nobody can. Period." She frowns.

"There are days when I can complete a perfume in a day and finish everything that was lying there piled up for three to four months in seconds. And there are days when I sit there exactly dead. You sit and nothing happens. The only thing that helps you is your belief in what you do."

I understand. The muse can be capricious, undependable. The professional knows that one cannot wait until moved by the spirit; one must slog it out no matter what.

"Anyone who creates has insecurities," she continues. "In this business you have to understand and accept that you are dedicating yourself to creating something for somebody else. It is not for me."

"So you need a little humility?" I ask.

"A lot of humility," she corrects. "Man, you face humiliation every day." She ground her cigarette into an ashtray.

"Perfumery is not taking a rose and a hyacinth and a lilac and putting it together to make a wonderful bouquet. If it were that easy I would be making 10,000 successful fragrances a day.

"You want the flowers to be like lovers. They should combine in an emotional way. Otherwise the fragrance is jagged. You need a floral wetness. A dewy kind of feeling. *Muguet*, or lily of the valley as it is commonly known, the most innocent flower, is great for that.

"But you will not find many lilacs dominating in fragrances, because lilac is potent and distinctive. It will take over."

So how does Sophia Grojsman create a fragrance?

"You see pictures in your head," she explains to me. "Think of standing by the ocean. Your mind immediately goes there. You think fish and sand and wind and salt air. Or think of something you want to eat. A piece of chocolate cake. You immediately sense it; you can almost taste it; the saliva flows. It's the same way with making perfume. I have these images and I try to realize it by putting the right ingredients together."

Like a poem or a painting, a perfume takes shape inside the mind. "You dream your fragrance," Jean Kerleo had said. There is a transcendent magic in the process of creation. Edmond Roudnitska created the intensely floral fragrance Femme, in 1943, during the worst days of the war, in a building with a rubbish dump on one side and a paint factory on the other.

Grojsman pulls out another cigarette and lights it. "I build my fragrances from bottom to top. Like a pyramid. In layers. It's geometric. In some fragrances, some orientals, for example, you get an immediate flush of a top note, and then it grows. Others might have a slower, smoother unfolding."

I comment that her description of the structure of a fragrance reminds me of music composition, and how long a note is held.

"Yes. The art closest to what I do is music," she agrees.

"Compare your perfumes to an opera. Which one would it be?"

Grojsman laughs. "*Carmen.* I want every woman to be mysterious and ardent. I have this urge to be alive. To be somebody. I'm a gypsy by nature. I *am* Carmen."

My inability to create a fragrance and the artistry of a Sophia Grojsman or Jean Kerleo have absolutely nothing to do with the physique of my nose. Give or take a few hundred thousand, a perfumer has the same number of nasal neurons as you and I—about three to five million per nostril, or six to ten million total. Perfumers and the rest of us start on a level playing field.

What perfumers have that you and I do not is the skill of olfactory concentration and focus; perfumers can smell, and then mentally dissect a fragrance. Because of their creativity, they can dream a fragrance. Because of years of study and training, they can create one.

The fraternity (and sorority: women, an increasing presence, represent about 20 percent of the perfumers working in the field today) is an elite one. In the world, there are only about 400 or so perfumers; more than half work in the United States. In this country at least, they are, literally, about one in a million.

"In the old days you became a perfumer because you were born into a perfume family," explains Henri Pailhes, studies manager of the school of perfumery in Versailles— the *Institut Supérieur International du Parfum, de la Cosmétique et de l'Aromatique Alimentaire* (ISIPCA). "The perfumer would say to his son—and it was always the son—'now you're going to start learning how to be a perfumer.' Today, we have a more democratic system." Even so, competition is fierce; the school accepts only 50 of the 600 or so students who apply.

At ISIPCA perfumers-to-be start their studies about the age of 18 to 20. They'll spend the first year learning the raw materials in relentless drills. Then they'll learn how to smell and how to develop a vocabulary of fragrance. They'll also study the classic perfumes and the different categories of fragrance. They'll learn the chemistry of fragrance and how to put a scent together. And, during the course of their study, the perfumers will do apprenticeships, work-study programs, with companies in the fragrance business so they'll get hands-on experience in the real world.

"I was 13 when I decided to become a perfumer," recalls Rodrigo Flores-Roux, a 1991 graduate of the school, and now a perfumer at Quest in New York City. "I began collecting perfume bottles. And then I began smelling what was inside the bottles. I started to recognize the different fragrances. I was like a bloodhound, smelling everyone. It must have been

The finishing touch for a bottle of Joy by Jean Patou, a lush mix of the finest French jasmine and rose, is a
hand-tied, gold-leaf cord. The production of the perfume remains something of a craft. Each woman working in
the small factory where the perfume is bottled can trim and finish only 250 such bottles a day. The less costly
eau de parfum is handled by an automated process. The black and red flacon, designed in 1932, was inspired
by an antique jade snuff bottle. Joy, touted as the world's costliest perfume, debuted in 1930.

ABOVE *"We fill by hand, not pump," explains one of the women who works in the factory in a Paris suburb where Joy, a prestige perfume, is bottled one-by-one. "We don't want to risk oxidation."* FOLLOWING PAGES *Jean Kerleo, chief perfumer at Jean Patou, is the steward and guardian of Joy's excellence, but also a creator of new fragrances. "A perfume is like a beautiful dress," he says. "You feel better for wearing it."*

annoying for a 13-year-old kid to sniff around people and tell them, 'You're wearing this. You're wearing that.'"

Flores-Roux, a native of Mexico, studied biology but left the university at the age of 20, before graduation, because he'd been accepted by the perfumery school. "There was no point in me staying and counting the legs of insects," he said. "I knew I wanted to be a perfumer." As an assignment during his first year of perfumery school he was asked to duplicate the smell of muguet, or lily of the valley. But lily of the valley doesn't grow in Mexico. He had never smelled the flower he was asked to replicate, and would not have the chance to smell it for six months. It was autumn. Muguet would not bloom until spring.

"I saw my first muguet in May," he recalled. "A friend, also a perfumer, bought me a plant growing in a little pot. I still have that sprig of flower. I keep it bound in a book. To this day, I have a special affection for muguet. I think it is wonderful."

Even after three years of study at ISIPCA students are only technicians, Henri Pailhes says. To be a perfumer—to really understand how to put a fragrance together—can take five, ten, fifteen years of long, hard work.

"The big stars are few and far between," he says. "If we produce one Edmond Roudnitska, I would be pleased. I tell students: 'Not everyone can be a soloist. But you can still play in the orchestra.'"

The orchestra includes perfumers who formulate fragrances for household products—soaps, detergents, air fresheners, cat litter, shaving cream, fabric softeners, trash bags, diapers—which is the high-volume end of the industry. Although the profit margin is not as pronounced as in fine fragrance, a soap or detergent, which may use several million pounds of fragrance a year, can make more money for a supplier than a perfume.

The glamour and prestige belong to the estimated 20 percent of perfumers who work on fine fragrances. "It's the difference between doing haute couture, and say, a line of shorts for JCPenney," says a woman in the fragrance industry. "No one is saying I want to tingle the senses of the woman doing the wash."

Well, not quite—the soap and detergent makers do hope to tingle the senses of the woman doing the wash. After all, that's a highly competitive market as well. But I sense an unspoken hierarchy between fine fragrance and household product perfumers. "Not long ago you could do both if you wanted to," Thierry Wasser, of Firmenich, says. "Some still do. Now we are becoming specialized. Now you usually do fine fragrance or household products. If you do fine fragrance, you do mass or prestige. Next we'll be specialized into masculine and feminine."

He continues. "Fine fragrance perfumers are part of the fashion industry. We dress in our Armani suits and wear our preppy shoes. *The look* is important."

In truth, Wasser says, the household perfumer's job is more difficult. "Our base in fine fragrance is alcohol. It's easy to work with. Their base is stink—ammonia, soap powder, bleach. Imagine how you have to think about the life of your fragrance. If you do a detergent, it has to smell good in the box, in the washing machine, after the dryer, when you iron, and in the closet.

"The household product guys are excellent poker players. Their smell is a lie. They have to trick the nose." Wasser means they have to mask noxious smelling substances. You can be sure that a liquid strong enough to clean the tile floor of your bathroom is going to smell awful. "It is very sophisticated the work they do," Wasser says. "They don't need *the look*."

It takes five, ten, fifteen years to make a perfumer, Henri Pailhes of the perfumery school in Versailles had said. In spring I go to Grasse, France, to learn perfumery in three days. Of course, I won't actually learn perfumery in three days, but Françoise Marin, director of Givaudan Roure's school of perfumery, assures me I will learn some of the basics. "You will work hard," she warns.

The school, which has since moved to the Paris suburb of Argenteuil, is located about three miles from the town of Grasse in a cream-colored stone building with a red-tiled roof, a former hospital-turned-monastery-turned-factory dating back to the 17th century. The Givaudan Roure school, unlike the government-sponsored ISIPCA in Versailles, is company-run. Its purpose is to develop talent in-house. Once upon a time, many of the big suppliers ran their own perfumery schools. The Givaudan Roure school is possibly the last of its kind.

The setting is picture-perfect. More precisely, the setting is olfactory-perfect. Grasse is the traditional home of perfumery. The city practically breathes fragrance. Walk through the narrow cobblestone streets of the old town and you are bathed in scent. A restaurant door opens, releasing a cloud of saffron, tomato, and garlic. Confectionery shops display trays of candied rose and violet petals and a tiny fragrant almond cookie called a *calisson d'Aix*. In the patisserie you may buy a *fougassette*, a flat bread made with orange-blossom-water, or a *navette*, an orange blossom water cookie. The sharp, acrid smell of espresso mingles with the licorice of *pastis* in cafes. Everything not redolent of is, at least, reminiscent of scent. The stucco and stone buildings are painted in ice-cream colors such as tangerine, lemon, and raspberry. Geraniums spill from window boxes. And on a summer night the wind carries the rich, warm scent of jasmine.

On a morning in May I take my place in a conference room with about half a dozen others. They are Givaudan Roure clients who work for a Swiss chain of stores called Migros. Our compressed course is a special arrangement for clients, a serious attempt to educate them about the inside workings of perfumery.

Françoise Marin, a tall woman with a swirl of frosted hair and features exaggerated by makeup and large glasses, begins by telling us something about herself. Her father was a manager of Charabot, a supplier of raw materials to the industry based in Grasse. As a child she would put geranium leaves in bottles filled with water in hopes of creating a perfume. "I must try that again this summer," she muses. Later she became a perfumer, and in 1991 became director of the Givaudan Roure school, founded

in 1947 to provide in-house training for the companies' own perfumers.

The happy combination of mild weather and fine soil made Grasse ideal for growing the flowers of perfume, Marin explains to us. So, when Catherine de Médicis introduced the fashion for scented gloves in the 16th century, Grasse, already a center of leather production, was poised to take center stage in the world of fragrance.

"Unfortunately, I cannot still say it is the capital of perfume," she says, explaining that greed replaced mercantile shrewdness; family-run businesses became top-heavy; squabbles erupted; profits dropped; and factories folded. Before 1900 there were 78 major fragrance houses in Grasse. Today, there are five.

Marin is a *Grassoise*, a native of Grasse, and in her voice you can hear a mixture of love and hate for her town, the kind of sadness one harbors for a lover, who has slowly, almost imperceptibly, changed into someone you'd rather not know.

She summons for us the spirit of three perfumers who have influenced her. Jean Carles, founder of the school, whose nose was insured for three million dollars. Germaine Cellier, one of the first women in the field, who smoked heavily and lived hard but created magnificent fragrances like Vent Vert, Fracas, and Jolie Madame. And Edmond Roudnistka, the celebrated perfumer and creator of Eau Sauvage and Miss Dior, who spoke of his flowers with such love you might have thought he was speaking of a woman.

"What does a perfumer need?" she asks rhetorically, then answers the question herself. "Curiosity, curiosity, curiosity."

It is day one. We begin the perfumer's drill: learning the different materials of fragrance. We're handed small vials with different oils and a package of blotters. We'll start off easy. There are only 27 notes to learn on the first round. To learn these scents, we are instructed to associate each one with a memory and jot down the association in a small notebook.

Tuberose: *Toothpaste*, I write.

Oakmoss. *Seaweed that has been shut up in a closet for weeks.*

The blotter dipped in cassis makes me wince. It smells like stale urine, although Caroline, one of Françoise's second-year students, tells me that a slight touch makes her think of kir.

Distinguishing between neroli and petitgrain oil is tricky. Both come from different parts of the same plant, the bigaradier, or bitter orange tree, which grows in southern Spain. Neroli oil, distilled from the flower, smells the sweetest. Petitgrain, distilled from the leaves, is heavier. The tree supplies yet a third oil, bitter orange oil, from the fruit peel.

Citronella reminds me of a vacation in the Caribbean: The small bungalow filled with a fog of mosquitoes as we made a gallant attempt to ward off the insect invasion by burning citronella candles.

By the time I get to vetiver (*a bag of peanuts, the circus*) the scents begin to blur. Hadn't Jean Carles, the founder of this school, said such tedium was "absolutely necessary. Could a musician write a symphony without ever having practiced scales?"

After the Swiss clients leave in late afternoon I remain behind to practice in the laboratory with the real students. It is strange to think of all the romance and beauty that can be created in such a severe-looking place. There are bare tables on three sides of the room and on the fourth, a glass-walled cabinet filled with glass bottles, two measuring scales, and boxes of tiny vials. Every perfume starts out this way: an idea, a piece of paper, a clutch of glass bottles, a measuring scale.

Since the bottles are labeled in French, Caroline helps find the oils for me. Jasmine—*jasmin*, in French, is easy to find; *girofle clous* (cloves) and *mousse de chêne* (oakmoss) are not.

Caroline is 22 years old, but with a seriousness and determination that belies her age. She tells me she is from Mouans-Sartoux, a village five miles from Grasse.

"So you are a *Grassoise?*" I say.

"Oh no," she remonstrates. "To be a *Grassoise*, you have to be born, live, and die here."

I settle down and start smelling. Tuberose. *Toothpaste.* Oakmoss. *Seaweed.* Vetiver. *Peanuts.*

"Do you ever get bored with this?" I ask Celine, another student.

"Bored by smelling?" she replies, a note of incredulity in her voice.

The white blotter dipped in jasmine oil emerges brown in color, a contrast from the colorlessness of other oils. I triumphantly make a note, figuring if all else fails I can identify it by the distinctive stain.

Jasmine. *Brown.*

Caroline looks at me reprovingly when I point this out.

"That is not a good way to do it. You don't look. You *smell*," she says.

I ask Caroline, who is going through the same exercise but with a more complicated series of notes, why she became a perfumer.

"My younger sister cannot smell," she tells me. "And so my mother was always very attentive to my ability to smell. She would cook and say, 'smell this . . . smell that.' I think that is why I decided to become a perfumer."

On day two we learn accords, a balanced combination of several notes blended together to make a single impression. The difference between a note and an accord is like the difference between the single G note and a G-sharp chord in music.

We're given four bottles filled with different chemicals, a scale, an eyedropper, and several empty bottles. The chemicals—phenylethyl alcohol, lyral, geraniol, and galaxolide—will, when mixed together in exactly the right proportions, produce the scent known as Rose de Noel 1267/B, a synthetic rose accord.

Françoise explains that phenylethyl alcohol is the main

Marie Aude Couture, Nicolas Anorga, and Yuri Endo learn some of the thousands of notes they must commit to memory during their time as students at the Givaudan Roure school of perfumery in Grasse, France. Such drills are only the beginning. It takes years of study, then many more years of practice to produce a master perfumer.

component of the accord: It's the rose-ness of the rose. Lyral gives freshness; geraniol adds pleasantness and roundness. And galaxolide, a musky note, will make the accord smooth and long lasting.

We're divided into two teams. It's up to us to figure out the proportions and produce the accord.

My team gets down to work and begins to experiment. Since none of us seems to be mathematical geniuses, and because it's easier to work in units of ten, we decide to divide the formula into ten parts. It's obvious we won't need much of the musky note provided by galaxolide, so we decided that one part—or 10 percent of the whole—should suffice. But the other ingredient percentages aren't so easy to figure out. Making an accord turns out to be like cooking. Instead of tasting and saying, "Too much salt," you smell and decide "too musky" or "not musky enough." On trial two, more by sheer luck than anything else, we hit the right combination: four parts phenylethyl, two parts lyral, three parts geraniol, one part galaxolide. We present our finished accord to Marin. She sniffs the vial and beams approvingly. Jackpot! Instead of three cherries on the slot machine, it's three roses.

Our accord, Rose de Noel, one of many such rose accords, is a synthetic. By way of contrast Marin lets us smell real rose oil from the *rose de mai*, and talks about the gorgeous naturals that made Grasse famous—violet, rose, jasmine, lavender, orange blossom, and mimosa. "The difference between naturals and synthetic oils is like the difference between polyester and silk," she tells us.

On day three Marin passes out a brief. In this exercise we are to play the role of suppliers competing for a new fragrance. It's our job, Marin tells us, to interpret the brief, produce a fragrance, name it, design a package for it, and plan a marketing campaign. And by the way, she adds, come up with a name for your company.

We're divided into two teams: the men and the women. We silently scan the brief.

"For a man who is living everywhere and nowhere else," it reads. "He is between 25 and 40. You can meet him on Wall Street. Directing a movie. Running a farm. Playing golf in Puerto Rico the week after climbing on the Jungfrau. He likes to dance the Macarena with the famous top model Celia, but he also enjoys literature that he reads in his little house in the mountains of Montana with his old dog nearby. Launch day, February 14, Valentine's Day."

In a real competition we'd be given weeks or months to develop our submissions. Marin allows us 30 minutes. There is a concession. To save time, and in deference to our status as beginners, we're given six vials with premixed bases. A base is a mixture of chemicals; it's kind of like using a cake mix instead of starting from scratch. Instead of thousands of ingredients to agonize over we only have six. But the agony will exist nonetheless. We still have to figure out which of the six ingredients to use and in what proportion.

But first there is the matter of the brief. "The guy sounds weird," someone comments. "And the brief is so contradictory," adds another.

"That's how it is with briefs," Marin says with a shrug.

Our group meets and decides as a first order of business to name our company Avant Garde Fragrances. That's easy. Then we try to make sense of the brief, which is more difficult. There's the Montana ranch, mountain climbing in Switzerland, golf weekends, and the trophy girlfriend. Our hypothetical client-hero is clearly a bachelor, outdoorsy, filthy rich, and perhaps somewhat trashy in his tastes.

After heated discussion we decide the fragrance should have the freshness of lavender to give the impression of the outdoors, the sparkle of citrus to convey the idea of freedom, and a dash of warmth, supplied by musk, to speak to the playboy nature of our hypothetical client.

Svati Balik, one of my teammates, measures out drops from each of the vials, seeing if she can come up with an acceptable-smelling scent, while I, as the native English-speaking member of the group, jot down proposed names.

"Man About Town?" I suggest. My colleagues give a thumbs-down.

"Wall Street?" Too dull is the consensus.

"Escape?" Too bad. Calvin Klein got there first; the name is taken.

Finally, I propose the name Getaway ("the fragrance for the man who likes fast cars, fast living, fast women, and making fast exits," I suggest). We agree, and not a moment too soon. It's time for our presentation. We're summoned to an office adjoining the conference room, where Françoise Marin, who plays the role of client in this reversal of roles, confronts us, saying, "What do you have to show me?" We offer a blotter with a sample of our new, exciting fragrance for men: Getaway. What makes the exercise so delicious is that usually it's my classmates, who work for Migros, who are in the client seat and calling the shots. Now the tables are turned.

"Too sweet," Marin opines. She gives us 20 minutes to come up with a modification as well as a viable packaging concept.

We go back to the conference room, makeshift headquarters for the Avant Garde Fragrances team. First we work on revising the formula. We decide to add more lavender, which will freshen the scent and make it less sweet, and cut back on the musky notes. Now, what about packaging? Should the bottle be frosted glass or transparent? What about a Plexiglas-like plastic flask, someone asks? Too cheap looking, is the consensus. A leather pouch? Too expensive; we'd blow the budget. Finally, we agree that transparency has more chic. We'll go with a clear glass bottle. But the bottle will have green accents on it, perhaps racing stripes or chevrons, and so will the cardboard box it's packaged in. After all, our hypothetical client is an outdoors-kind-of-guy. The fragrance itself will be transparent, too. We won't color it. And we'll offer a travel-sized bottle for those warm, balmy days on the Puerto Rican golf course.

I finish sketching the bottle just as we are called into Marin's office for our second presentation. When we finish, Marin, who has sat absolutely expressionless throughout the presentation, asks, "What about price?"

A dead silence. We've neglected to price out our product. I know my limitations. Numbers are not my thing. I turn to Svati Balik, one of my team members. "I'm creative. You're marketing," I say.

She comes to the rescue. "We envision our fragrance as top of the line. Eighty dollars a pound," she says crisply.

Marin is expressionless. "I'll let you know," is her dead-pan response.

A word about pricing. Suppliers sell their oils to clients by the pound. This is the price for pure oil—the client can then dilute that concentration accordingly: 22 percent for a perfume, less for an eau de toilette or cologne. Mass market fragrances sell for about $30 a pound. High-end prestige scents sell for about $60 to $80 a pound. A few sell for more. With a handful of exceptions, by the time a pound of oil is diluted into its proper concentration and bottled, the cost of the actual "juice," as it is known in the industry, adds up to a few dollars—sometimes less.

"Take a product like a car that sells for $40,000," Geoffrey Webster, of Givaudan Roure, had explained in an interview in Teaneck, New Jersey, several months earlier. "There's probably not more than $1,300 worth of steel being used in that car, yet that car is steel. The price is not about the raw material. It's the total package that goes into the car." He reached for a package of Bijan perfume behind his desk. "Look at that beautiful carton. Imagine what that costs—the liner, the label, the cap, the cap liner, the label on the bottle, the glass itself, the coating underneath it, the expense in producing the bottle. Profits are not outrageous in this industry."

Our deadline is up. The two competing groups gather in the conference room to hear Françoise Marin's verdict. We discover that our competitors, the Chaotic Perfume Company, have submitted a fragrance called Rainbow Man. It's Getaway versus Rainbow Man. May the best fragrance win. "This business is win/lose, there's nothing in between," a Givaudan Roure vice president had explained to me earlier. Now I see his point. This competition is make-believe, but I find myself uncharitably hoping we trample our rivals—big time.

Françoise Marin consults her notes and makes the announcement: Getaway, the submission from Avant Garde Fragrances, wins. In the real world the champagne corks would start popping. But we're not done yet. Marin calls us into yet another conference to complain about our pricing. Can't we come down? What about a discount?

"No way," we answer. "This is an expensive fragrance to produce."

Then, to our astonishment, she demands immediate delivery of 20 tons. "We need it right away. Right away," she says. "The advertising campaign is in progress. We want to be on the market now. So hurry. Hurry."

I feel a headache coming on. Twenty tons is a big order to turn around in such a short time. But we've won the contract. We will meet the demand. After all, our job is to please the client.

"Do you have all the materials in stock?" Marin pushes. "What about a certificate that the ingredients meet all the client's requirements and the latest regulations? If you can get the oil to us early . . ."

By now I have as the French say, *un grand mal de tête*. But never mind my head; I discover I lack an industrial-strength stomach. The business world is not for me.

I decide to keep the job I have.

To cradle the Elizabeth Arden perfume It's You, Baccarat created this crystal flacon in 1939. Such exquisite presentations, the collaborative result of perfumer, designer, and glassmaker, enhance the appeal and marketability of a scent. The notion of designing a flacon for a specific fragrance came into its own in the 19th century.

FOUR

A Bed of Roses

I like to think of perfume as the breath of flowers—but not just flowers. Perfume is made from roots of iris and ginger; seeds of anise or coriander; leaves of laurel or geranium; peels of orange, lemon, and grapefruit; resins like balsam, olibanum (better known as frankincense) or galbanum, an Asian gum that actually stinks until the perfumers start working their magic. Some 200 plants are reportedly raised commercially for their use in perfume. Of course perfume also calls upon, albeit infrequently, animal products, and, ever increasingly, synthetics, but for now let's keep our focus floral.

The geography of perfume is an itinerary of the exotic. The sweet, white flower of the ylang-ylang can be found growing in the Comoros Islands, off the coast of east Africa. For patchouli, go to Indonesia. India grows the most heavenly sandalwood. For the herbal mustiness of oakmoss? Yugoslavia. Cloves? Tanzania. Vanilla beans? Madagascar. Orange oil from the Ivory Coast; lime oil from Mexico. Mandarin from Sicily. Rose from Turkey, Morocco, and Bulgaria. Jasmine from India, Egypt, and France. To create a perfume is to travel by proxy.

"Once I smelled jasmine in a dream. It was absolutely unmistakable," Ilias Ermenidis, a perfumer, told me. His voice was touched with wonder, as if he still couldn't believe it had happened. Such a scent is unforgettable and intoxicating. There is magic in the richness of jasmine, the voluptuousness of orange blossom, and the sweetness of that most romantic of blooms—the rose. The "Queen of Flowers," Sappho, the Greek poet, called it. It is, we may read, found as a main ingredient in three-fourths of all modern prestige perfumes, such as Paris, Eternity, Trésor, and not to mention classics like L'Air du Temps, Joy, and Chanel No. 5.

The Arabs discovered how to distill petals and produce rose water, which they used in perfume and to scent food. They learned that flowers plunged into boiling water release their oil into the steam, which, when run through a loop of tubing and cooled, condenses into a layer of rose water on the bottom and oil on top. Beginning in 810 A.D. the caliphs of Baghdad received 30,000 bottles of rose water as an annual tribute from Persia. The grandeur of the rose was compared with that of kings. "Each of us is worthy of the other," a Caliph proclaimed. Only a Persian mogul could—and did—fill the canals of his garden with rose water.

A shower of roses falls from the hands of a picker in Bulgaria's Valley of Roses.
The arithmetic of roses can be daunting: Two tons of petals produce a pound of Bulgarian rose oil.

ABOVE Purple waves of lavender roll across Provence, France. Though cutting machines now do the work on most lavender farms, smaller, older fields lack sufficient room for tractors to maneuver and must be harvested by hand. FOLLOWING PAGES One of the few farmers who harvests lavender this way, Gilbert Gouin holds a sickle, the tool his workers use from dawn to dusk during lavender season. Once cut, lavender is bound into sheaves to dry before processing.

By the 10th century the process of distillation had probably been introduced to Europe, perhaps by way of Spain.

To speak of roses is to speak of romance. The Greek courtesan Aspasia, who lived in Miletus in the 5th century B.C., kept her house suffused in a perfume of rose and aloe, a scent reportedly so beguiling a visitor would float in an Elysian stupor. The 16th-century Arab book of erotica, *The Perfumed Garden*, advises a man planning a seduction, to fill his tent with perfumes, among them the scent of roses. "And I will make thee beds of roses," promises "The Passionate Shepherd to His Love" in Christopher Marlowe's 16th-century poem. A grower's association reports that 98 million roses were sold for Valentine's Day, 1997, in the United States.

Why does a rose smell so sweet? To make it simple: The chemical that grabs the nose and screams *rose!* is an organic compound known as phenylethyl alcohol, but other components, namely citronellol, geraniol, nerol, and damascenone, add to the heady scent.

What we refer to as the scent of a rose is a vapor, the result of oil droplets found in petals that evaporate and find their way to the nose. Examine this vapor and you find clusters of molecules made up of hydrogen, oxygen, and carbon. In this world of organic chemistry—the branch of science concerned with carbon compounds—how these elements bond together determines what the nose smells. Link this trio one way and you get the scent of Bulgarian rose; shuffle the molecular deck slightly and you have the scent of the diminutive wild rose snaking up the trellis in your backyard. Another shuffle and you might end up with the scent of vinegar. So a chemist will tell you that the pear-like sweetness and intensity of Bulgarian rose comes from a compound called damascenone, while the heavier, dark, richness of Moroccan rose comes from its high percentage of phenylethyl alcohol. But to peer at molecules through the lens of science is only one way of looking at a rose.

In May, the season of roses in France, I visit Grasse. Surely the most celestial of roses is the *rose de mai*—the rose of May.

The soil of Provence, mild weather, and blooms of *Rosa centifolia*, as the species is known to botanists, conspire to produce an absolute of exquisite delicacy.

"Like fine wine," says Joseph Mul, owner of 12 acres of rose fields near Grasse, snuggled in a valley between the French Alps and the Mediterranean Sea.

Mul, a large, round man with an equally rotund, beaming face, shows me his fields, where women are harvesting flowers. "The roses are picked as soon as they are ready," Mul says. "Not a second before or after." He plucked a rose from a candelabra of branches. "Just opened," he said with a smile of satisfaction. He handed me a pale pink bloom. I tucked it in a buttonhole.

A worker can pick 2,100 rose blossoms an hour—about 13 pounds' worth—Mul tells me, keeping close watch on the women at work in his fields. "It takes 800 kilos of roses to produce one kilo of absolute. Unfortunately this isn't a good year. There are only six to seven blooms per branch. Sometimes we have as many as 25."

"Why?" I ask.

"*Le temps.* Weather. Spring was cold and it hardly rained, which slowed growth. The harvest will be 20 percent less." He looked mournful.

Weather is not the only thing that can go wrong. Mul ticks off a couple of potential ailments: "Rust (a fungus), insects like green flies and beetles." He might have added the usual conspiracies of nature: too much rain, too little, too soon, too late, too hot, too cold. "Believe me, I have to be on hand all the time," Mul tells me. "I check up on these roses every day. I wouldn't dream of leaving the work to anyone else." The stakes are high. "Say I wanted to start a new field of roses," he continued. "It would take three years to bring a rose to flower and cost me $55,000."

For now the investment makes sense; Chanel contracts to buy every petal he can produce. "Look ahead ten years," I say. "Will these fields still be here?"

"Who knows?" he replies. "I'm not the one to ask." Whether a market for his roses will remain depends on how long companies like Chanel will be willing to pay for the

costly absolute, which currently sells for $3,650 a pound. "The most important thing for a farmer is to earn a living," Mul says. "If it's not worth growing, I won't grow it.

"We've always moved with the times," he continues. "My grandfather was the first to bottle milk in this region. In the middle of the 19th century Cannes was a resort for the British. My grandfather advertised in the Cannes newspapers that each child could come and pick out his or her own cow, and get a bottle of milk delivered each morning from their own special cow." When that market dried up his grandfather raised sheep, then switched to field crops, like roses.

"When I was a boy there were no houses out there at all," Mul says, indicating the valley below with its cascade of houses and condominiums. "If you were a little taller you'd see even more. Just after the war there were 50 farmers here. Today, there are only five. If my grandparents could come back and see this they wouldn't recognize any of it."

"Do you feel like an endangered species?" I asked.

A Gallic shrug. "I am."

Mul's roses are not distilled—a process that relies on boiling petals in water and condensing the steam to produce an oil. At his on-site factory the extraction process coaxes the essence from the fragrant blooms. Extraction, a more gentle process than distillation, relies on chemical solvents. Extraction is the preferred process for flowers like jasmine and mimosa, which are too delicate for the high temperatures of distillation. In extraction petals are layered on plates of perforated metal, lowered into a vat to which a solvent is added, and heated. The solvent dissolves the oils, waxes, and pigments in the petals. Next the mixture is piped into a still, where it evaporates into a waxy substance called a concrete, which, when dissolved in alcohol and filtered, produces the pure, concentrated essence known as an absolute. In general an absolute is heavier and has more body than an oil, which is lighter and has more lift to it. Another method of processing flowers for oil called enfleurage is no longer used. In enfleurage jasmine or other flowers were meticulously embedded petal by petal on glass plates layered with animal fat. The fat absorbed the fragrance, just as a stick of butter left next to a clove of garlic absorbs that odor. The scent-impregnated fat was then processed to yield oil.

It was ten o'clock in the morning. The sun had begun to wilt the flowers, marking the end of that day's harvest. Mul paused by a cluster of tightly clenched buds. "By tomorrow they'll be open and we begin again.

"Picking roses will never be done by machine," he commented. "Labor is 60 percent of the cost and makes the difference between the price of rose in Grasse and in Morocco. What I pay for a day's work here is worth a month's work there."

"Do you dream of roses at night?"

"No, I just collapse in bed."

Just then a gust of wind lifted the rose from my buttonhole, sending it to the ground.

Mul picked it up and flicked it into a burlap bag. "I never waste a single petal," he said.

A continent away, in the south of Morocco where the Atlas Mountains taper down to the Sahara Desert, roses thrive by grace of snowmelt from the peaks. The region is an expanse of rock and sand the color of an orange rind that has baked too long in the sun. The horizon remains unbroken except for a stray herd of camels or the skeletal limbs of a spindly shrub. Driving through such lonely and arid land, the Gouna Valley, a ribbon of green unfurling between mountains, materializes as a mirage. That roses should grow in such a place seems nothing short of a miracle.

It is a small-scale miracle to be sure. The valley is a slim two to four miles wide on either side of the taupe-colored Gouna River and only 40 miles long. For those who live here education and income is minimal. The houses with their filigree of wrought-iron windows are made of mud. In this valley one's livelihood is, most often, a matter of soil and water. There is wheat and corn, figs, apricots, almonds, peaches, and even olives. And there are, above all, roses. The rose crop, harvested and processed in the space of four

India's jasmine industry is centered near the village of Virapandi, where companies such as Nesstate Flora grow fields of Jasminum grandiflorum, *the species most used in perfumery. Women gather blossoms from 5:30 to 9:30 in the morning, the brief window of opportunity when the flowers remain open and their scent peaks. Known in India as "moonlight of the grove," jasmine blooms at night and closes during the day.*

weeks or so, is worth nearly a million dollars. It is a significant sum of money for such a modest place. In spring, by way of celebration, there is a festival dedicated to the rose with dancing and feasting and an influx of tourists.

In El Kelâa des M'Gouna, the dusty town at the heart of this region, the flower entwines itself around daily life—ushering men and women through joy and sorrow, sickness and health, life and death. "Infant rash can be soothed by ground rose powder," an old man told me. We were standing in a shed where flowers were brought in to be weighed, and as he spoke he reached into a sack, pulled out a handful of blooms, and held them to his face as though devouring their scent. "During festivals women mix petals with henna and put this in their hair," he said, adding that the cure for digestive troubles was pigeon tajine, made with rose water, and that an infected eye could be treated with rose petal paste mixed with thyme and olive oil. "And when someone dies," the old man concluded, letting the petals fall from his hands, "they wash him in rose water, dress him in white, and cover his body with roses."

Several miles down the road, in the corrugated tin-roofed factory where flowers are taken for processing, I sank back onto a bed of roses. Joseph Mul would have been appalled. It was the end of the harvest and the men had, for my delight and also to make sure the petals wouldn't overheat and ferment before they could be processed, spread the contents of dozens of 65-pound sacks of roses out onto the factory's cement floor. The petals—there must have been a ton—would be swept up and shoveled into vats for extraction, but for the moment they were spread out for me to luxuriate in.

As though in a fantasy I covered myself with roses as the Romans did. Roses—*damascena:* the rose cultivated by early Arab perfumers—rained down on my head. They were piled in my lap and had become entangled in my hair. The scent was intoxicating.

It was an extravagance, this carpet of roses, for the crop that year had been disappointing. The *cherguir,* the wind that swoops down from the snow-topped Atlas Mountains, had touched the flowers with killing frost, reducing the amount of flowers that could be used for oil.

Yet, in fields on either side of the river the Berber women in their indigo gowns were pleased. The price of rose oil had risen, and the wages paid for harvesting—four dirhams a kilogram (about 50 cents)—were higher than the year before. "Many thorns this year," a woman, who gave her name as Zahra, said as she plucked the blossoms. Her sweet face, encircled by a flowered scarf, was furrowed by sun and hard work. "But the price is up so I don't care. Would that the harvest never ends."

As I watched, she came to the hedge that marked the division between two fields, and carefully kept to her half of the hedge, as if it were bisected by an invisible line. "Should my hand stray too far over," Zahra explained, "my husband will say: 'Careful. Allah is watching.'"

And how would she spend her earnings?

She gave a thin smile in response. "We make the money," she said, moving on to another hedge. "The men spend it."

After the sacks were filled they would be carried to a concrete shed weighing station, one of dozens in the region. By the end of the morning Zahra would have picked five to ten pounds of roses, earning, at most, about five dollars. The sacks would be hoisted on a scale and carefully weighed, and wages would be paid accordingly.

"And we check," said the man in his long, white djellaba, tending the scale at Post 42, "to see that the petals are dry, not damp." His dark, hooded eyes scanned the contents of a sack that was about to be weighed.

"We do not," he said, quite firmly, "pay for water."

The arithmetic of flowers is easy to compute. The price of Joseph Mul's *rose de mai absolue* is $3,650 a pound. The price of Moroccan rose from the fields of El Kelâa des M'Gouna is $600 a pound. The difference in price explains a major change in the trade of essential oils: Provence was once the source of many wonderful oils such as rose, jasmine, lavender, and orange blossom, but today most major raw materials used in perfumery come from developing countries. Land in Provence has become too costly for flowers; condominiums and vacation homes have sprouted where roses once grew. High labor costs also add to the burden. So the business has shifted to countries like Bulgaria, Turkey, and Morocco.

The same economic reality that has uprooted rose fields in France has done the same to jasmine. In 1975 nearly 412 pounds of jasmine absolute were processed in the Grasse region. By 1996 this had dropped to about 60 pounds; so companies are switching to more prevalent and less costly jasmine from elsewhere. Only three perfume houses today use French jasmine at all—Chanel, Guerlain, and Jean Patou. Commercial cultivation of jasmine has moved to Egypt, Morocco, and India, where land and labor are less expensive. Only one large field of jasmine remains in Provence. It, too, belongs to Joseph Mul and its survival is not guaranteed.

"You must come back in September for the jasmine," said Françoise Marin, director of the School of Perfumery run by Givaudan Roure in Grasse. She handed me a blotter dipped in *absolue jasmin de Grasse*. It was rich, lush—the evocation of tropical nights heavy with the scent of flowers. In his *Natural History*, Pliny wrote of the belief that trees smell sweet where a rainbow has touched them. Surely, I thought, some such magic has touched these flowers.

She spoke of herself as a child of six, playing in the factory managed by her father, jumping in jasmine up to her waist. "Like landing in feathers," she said, her eyes filling with tears. "And the scent . . . " There was silence as she relived the memory. "I cannot describe. The flowers themselves. Softer than silk. So delicate. Fragile. You hold a bloom in your hand, and in a few minutes it turns brown."

There are other jasmines, it is true. There is the smooth, sweet jasmine grown in Italy, the slightly animalic Egyptian jasmine, and the even more animalic jasmine from India. But there is nothing so subtle, so fine, or as expensive and rare as jasmine from Grasse. A worker in Provence can earn about seven dollars a pound—maybe 22 times the wage earned by a worker in India—for harvesting the bloom. The delicate blossom must be picked so carefully that the most dexterous fingers can only gather 16 ounces of jasmine an hour.

French jasmine absolute, assuming you can find it, sells for $12,000 a pound. Indian jasmine absolute can be had for $500 a pound. *"Mais c'est de la merde,"* a perfumer told Françoise Marin 25 years ago when asked to use a cheaper jasmine. Even then it was dear, but you could still get it. Who could imagine it might disappear altogether?

The next day we drive by the Saint Donat Country Club where manicured greens have replaced the jasmine fields. "You'd think they could at least call it the Jasmine Country Club!" Françoise remarks. Then past the tiny town of Plascassier, engulfed by bedroom communities for Cannes and Nice. "Rose fields once. And now . . . " She huffed, expelling a puff of air between pursed lips. We drove on.

"You must come back for the jasmine," she repeats. "There is one large field left. One only. In five, ten years it will be gone." If it is gone the world will smell a little less sweet—for the exquisite scent of French jasmine will have vanished from the earth.

The trade in essential oils can be distilled down to the sound of the phone ringing in Dominique Goby's office in the town of Grasse. It's almost always ringing. It may be a Japanese client asking about the trend in patchouli pricing ("it will fall"), or a German client asking for a sample of lavender ("on the way"), or a customer in the United States asking for a quote on cypress oil ("60 dollars a kilogram").

FOLLOWING PAGES Jasmine is grown in India, Egypt, Italy, and France. Once France was the center of the essential oil industry, but rising costs of land and labor have shifted production to developing countries. French jasmine is a rare commodity these days and prohibitively expensive for all but a few prestige perfumes.

Two major varieties of rose are cultivated for the fragrance industry. OPPOSITE *The Rosa centifolia, or rose de mai, of Grasse, France, offers a lighter, sharper smell than the spicy richness of Rosa damascena, the Bulgarian damask rose. Roses are picked in the early hours to obtain the greatest possible amount of essence. As the morning unfolds, the oil yielded by the flowers drops.* ABOVE *Once picked, weighed, and bagged, the petals must be processed within 12 hours before they begin to wilt.*

As sales and marketing director for Systems Bio-Industrie, a processor and seller of perfumery oils, Goby watches some 60 different materials rise and fall in price. "Right now, I'm setting up my marketing campaign for rose oil," he explains, settling back into a black leather chair. Goby will offer buyers Moroccan, Bulgarian, Turkish, or a blend of rose oils. It is not, in his opinion, that Bulgarian rose oil is necessarily better than Moroccan or Turkish oils. It is a simply a matter of taste. "Like the difference between a Bordeaux and a Burgundy wine."

Just as grapes grown for wine, a rose grown for oil may vary in quality and quantity from year to year. The biggest variable is weather. To compensate for fluctuations in quality and quantity, a portion of each year's oil crop is often set aside and several years' crops blended together to even out the difference. The oil is stored in aluminum or stainless steel canisters and refrigerated at about 50°F to prevent degradation. A crop of roses, or any other plant, might also vary from one field to another depending on the exposure to sun and type of soil. Of course, to discern the difference between an oil from one area and the oil from another requires a nose of exquisite sensitivity. Jean Carles, a famous French perfumer whose career spanned more than 50 years, could tell the difference between a lavender oil from one field and that from another only two miles away.

"This year the price of roses in Morocco increased 20 percent," Goby says, explaining that an early frost killed off some of the flowers and resulted in a "short crop." Instead of an expected yield of a ton, the yield was only 1,540 pounds. "I may have to set quotas for our clients," Goby said. "I know I'll make some of them unhappy.

"I also spoke with a producer of rosemary. Morocco wants to cancel the rosemary harvest this year; the plant grows wild and the government feels it's being overharvested," Goby explained. He added, "I know the price will go up. We try to anticipate. I'll call my producer in Tunisia."

His two big worries are weather: "A typhoon in Réunion, an island off the coast of Madagascar, may ruin the geranium crop" and politics: "Take galbanum, a resin from a plant growing in Iran. When the ayatollah came into power the market collapsed. War in Somalia meant that olibanum, another resin used in perfumery, could not be collected. When the United States put an oil embargo on Haiti the stills that process vetiver, a grass that produces an oil with an earthy fragrance, went cold. We had to go to Indonesia instead."

Sometimes a small shortage translates into sheer speculative fever. "In November patchouli oil was $10 a pound. By April it had climbed to $30 a pound." Goby showed me a chart that looked like an EKG. "Of course it will drop again. Probably to $15 a pound by June. I tell clients: 'Wait if you can.'" Six months later, in November, when I check back Goby quotes the price of patchouli at $70 a pound. Instead of falling it has continued to climb. "I was wrong," he admits. "But I still think it will come down."

As the conversation continued a sweet smell wafted through the office from the factory behind Goby's office.

"What's being processed now?" I ask.

He leaned his head out the window. "Probably balsam."

I mention how haunting I found the scent of Grasse's jasmine.

"Of course." He nods. "The best jasmine comes from France. They say the more a plant suffers, the better the fragrance. Jasmine needs warmth. In Grasse we are almost on the edge of being too cold—not the case in Egypt or India.

"I remember as a boy driving home to Grasse from Cannes at night. The hills were totally covered with jasmine. The smell was incredible!"

"Do you miss the smell of jasmine at night?" I asked.

OPPOSITE TOP The journey from petal to perfume continues near Grasse, France, where rose petals are layered into multi-tiered metal plates for chemical extraction. The same process is used for jasmine flowers. BOTTOM In Kananj, India, sandalwood logs pass through the distillery, which extracts their oil.

He smiled. "I keep a little jasmine bush growing in my yard."

But the world of perfumery can't operate on natural oils alone. In the 1930s, says Geoffrey Webster, president of fragrances worldwide for Givaudan Roure, a perfume might be 85 percent natural, 15 percent chemical. Today it's the opposite.

Before 1890 perfumes were totally natural: They were simple floral waters with names like Violet of Parma or Coeur de Rose. "Figurative perfumes," Yves de Chiris of Quest calls them, meaning they are literal representations of flowers. Violet of Parma smells like violets. Coeur de Rose smells like roses. "The advent of synthetics allowed impressionism in perfumes," de Chiris says. Imagination could blossom. An abstract idea could find expression in a fragrance. Instead of a photograph of water lilies, think Monet. Instead of Coeur de Rose, think Chanel No. 5.

Synthetics also enable the replication of scents from flowers, like lilac and lily of the valley, that cannot be captured any other way. Synthetics are free from whims of weather and politics. They allow the use of scents from flowers too rare to be picked or from products, like musk, that would involve the killing of a wild animal.

If naturals give a perfume its richness and roundness, then synthetics represent the strength and backbone of a scent. Synthetics also give a fragrance its substantivity— the quality of lastingness. "Good fragrance is a balance between naturals and synthetics," says Harry Frémont, a perfumer. He has tried making perfumes exclusively from natural oils but, in his estimation, they fall flat. "They turn out dull and heavy," he says.

Aveda Corporation, the cosmetics company based in Minneapolis, Minnesota, is devoted to plant-derived oils. It calls its fragrances Pure-Fume and uses naturals in everything from lipsticks to shampoos. Synthetics in perfume? "I think from a biological and medical view they should be outlawed," Horst Rechelbacher, Aveda's CEO and chair, says. "You wouldn't eat toxins. Why inhale them?"

An allegiance to natural oils is not without sacrifice. "We are determined to use natural products but I know their weak points," confesses Aveda's chief perfumer, Koichi Shiozawa. "They're not long-lasting and there is limited variety. It is very difficult. But we feel we are working for a mission. We stick to nature." He ticks off a list of ingredients he is forbidden to use. "No animal notes, synthetic or otherwise, no aldehydes, no synthetic ambergris." Shiozawa sighs deeply. "Sometimes I feel like a perfumer in the 19th century. Every other perfumer has thousands of notes to work with. I only have several hundred. Oh, for a bit of musk. A hint of civet." Such animal notes, and nearly all are synthetic these days, anchor a perfume and allow it to last on the skin. Ambergris, also synthetically produced these days, gives a burnished glow to fragrances. The aldehyde that Shiozawa misses so much gives a perfume sparkle and life. Shiozawa places his hand on his heart as another sigh escapes his lips. "We must bid them a sad *adieu*."

Perfumery, like much else in life, is full of compromises. Natural oils are glorious, unspeakably romantic, and silken. But without synthetics the perfumer's palate is limited. No synthetics. No energy. No stability. No strength. Even so, says essential oil broker Dominique Goby, with the understanding that his bias and livelihood places him squarely on the side of natural oils, "At least for now a synthetic jasmine is still very far from the real thing."

As for me, I'll leave the chemists to their laboratory-grown molecules of phenylethyl alcohol and damascenone. Science is grand, but nature is grander still.

Make my bed of roses real.

Continuing the age-old tradition of courting divine favor with fragrance, flower vendors in Nilakkottai, India, leave a fragrant offering outside the temple of Ganesh, the elephant-headed god known as the "remover of obstacles" in the hope that the deity grants them a prosperous day.

FIVE

A Walk Through the Jungle

I am holding a pump-spray bottle the size and shape of a bottle of fingernail polish. The label reads Bari 85, code name for the scent of a flower identified as *Cavendishia quereme*. The flower, a dainty, trumpet-shaped bloom as red as a stoplight, grows on a leafy bush in the Costa Rican rain forest. The smell is pleasant, somewhere between peppermint candy-piquant and freesia-sweet.

It is too early to know how useful perfumers will find this particular fragrance, which may, or may not, find its way into anything from a perfume to a kitchen detergent. If its worth to perfumers remains uncharted, the wonder of its existence is not. Bari 85 is a scent taken from a flower that grows in a jungle deep in the green tangle of Costa Rica's interior. Until recently it was a fragrance unknown to perfumery. The scientists who found Bari 85 captured its scent without picking so much as a petal. They took nothing from the jungle but molecules. This scent's journey, from its jungle flower source to the small bottle in my hand, is a tribute to the sophistication of analytical and organic chemistry, those branches of science indispensable to the fragrance industry.

"The future of perfumery is in the hands of chemistry,"

said perfumer Ernest Beaux, creator of Chanel No. 5." We'll have to count on chemists to find new substances if we are to make new and original notes." Chemistry could not have a better advocate. Without the bracing overdose of alde-hyde, a synthetic chemical first produced in 1833, Beaux's exquisite perfume, Chanel No. 5, would lack luster. Other perfumers and their finest fragrances are similarly indebted. Without the dessert sweetness of vanillin, a synthetic vanilla created in 1877, Aimé Guerlain's perfume, Jicky, would not be nearly as luscious. Without the smoky-leather note of quinolines, a synthetic discovered in 1880, Germaine Cellier's edgily robust Bandit would collapse into tame dreariness.

There are other reasons for synthetics, or aroma chemicals as the industry prefers to call them. ("The word synthetic makes the industry squeamish," a scientist explained. "The connotations are bad.") Natural oils can vary in quality and quantity from year to year. Weather, soil, the plant itself and where it grows can affect the oil. Inconsistencies in essential oils can mean inconsistencies in a perfume. Synthetics ensure uniformity and circumvent the problem of availability. Synthetics help keep perfumes affordable

In the French Guianan rain forest, botanist Scott Mori pulls out-of-reach limbs in for a closer sniff. His audience below, Ken Purzycki and Tom McGee, are scientists who specialize in the chemistry of fragrance for Givaudan Roure, a supplier. They travel to remote corners of the world in search of new and exotic scents to excite the noses of sophisticated urban consumers.

because certain natural oils are out-of-reach expensive. Synthetic substitutes have, for the most part, replaced nearly all animal extracts, like musk, which is not obtained from a deer without killing it.

Then there's the zeitgeist factor. In the same way that tempera paints were suited to the crisply rendered, meticulously detailed, panels of the 13th-century Florentine artist Giotto, and enamel house paints were suited to the slap-dash 20th-century abstract forms of Jackson Pollock, the elements of perfume are often concordant to their era.

"Even if I could use them tomorrow, there are certain naturals I'm not even sure I'd go back to," says Claude Dir, a perfumer with Quest. "The ingredient you use has to be right for the time." The sweet, heavy floral perfumes of an earlier era depended on the sweet, heavy floral oils of *jasmin de Grasse, rose de mai,* and tuberose. Such lush, heavy notes may not be appropriate for today's sheer, clean, lighter fragrances.

Take dihydromyrcenol, a synthetic used originally to give a fresh, clean smell to soaps and detergents, for instance. It's inexpensive, extremely stable, and in recent years perfumers began adding it to fine fragrances like Davidoff's Cool Water and Joop!'s Nightflight. Added to floral and herbal notes, Dir explains, the material gives a tiny burst of citrus-like sparkle. It's the perfect finishing touch for a cool, fresh, transparent fragrance. Its use in fine fragrances coincided with the trend for light, bright scents. The time was right for the ingredient.

It's also a matter of balance. By themselves aldehydes are harsh; they smell like starched laundry. But used judiciously, aldehydes can lift and diffuse the most delicate florals, showing them off in the same way a well-crafted platinum mounting serves to frame the brilliance of a fine diamond. The moral of the story is that in perfumery there is no such thing as a bad odor. It's how—and with what else—a material is used.

A word about the stability of fragrances, and why perfumers need to know something about chemistry. Whether it's a single note like rose, or a complex perfume like Chanel No. 5, a fragrance in its most basic form is a molecular composition of carbon, oxygen, hydrogen, nitrogen, and sulfur.

Such molecules consist of atoms bonded together in an elaborate latticework. Bonds between atoms vary in strength. Think of school children playing snap the whip. Some will have a firmer grip than others—their part of the chain will most likely hold. Others, perhaps smaller and less strong, will have a more fragile hold—their part of the chain may break. Molecular links are similar. Molecules that contain atoms of carbon and hydrogen, are, in general, more stable than those containing oxygen, nitrogen, and sulfur. When exposed to light, heat, or simply the inexorable ticking of time, the handgrip between the less firmly anchored atoms can loosen and the compound decays.

Stability problems can surface at each step of the process. Take patchouli, for instance. If patchouli is distilled in an iron pot, rather than in a copper pot, the iron may leach out into the oil. Iron can ruin a fragrance; the element oxidizes and can turn a compound red—an undesirable event.

The perfumer would do well to know the nature of his chosen ingredients. He must factor in stability and use fragile materials sparingly, lest the gorgeous composition of his dreams be reduced to a bottle of sour, discolored waste.

And so the organic chemist is the perfumer's aide-de-camp. It's a relationship sometimes marked by misunderstanding, according to Luca Turin, a biophysicist and London-based scientist. He's passionate about perfume and was once hired by a major supplier to be an intermediary

PRECEDING PAGES The Costa Rican rain forest, with its profusion of flora and fauna, is a hothouse of scents never before used in perfumery. But not every find is appealing as a potential new note. "If we find three or four good flowers, we feel we've done really well," says Tom McGee. OPPOSITE An entire setting can become an element in perfumery, such as the smell of a tropical waterfall splashing over a vine-covered ledge. Perfumers sometimes join treks to experience firsthand new aromas in the wild.

between the two sides. "Perfumers tend to be frustrated by the fact that they cannot actually request a new smell to order from the chemists," he says. "By contrast, most chemists are frustrated when they come up with a really novel smell and the perfumers trash it because they can't think of what to do with it. Many raw materials languish for years on the shelf before a perfumer finds a way of using them."

A case in point is calone, a synthetic material patented in the 1970s with an oystery, marine-like scent. At first perfumers ignored it. "The note seemed weird," says Claude Dir. "Then briefs came in about seven or eight years ago asking perfumers to create fragrances with an oceanic freshness to them. Perfumers remembered it and said, 'Ah, we have this note.'" Today, calone plays a leading role in fragrances such as New West, Escape, and L'Eau d'Issey.

Several decades ago the fragrance industry adopted a new tool known as "headspace technology," which allowed chemists to capture an entire sensory experience. The term "headspace" comes from the process of brewing beer. Once upon a time a brew master would sniff the space just above the head, or foam, of the fermenting batch in order to tell whether the beer had fermented enough to be kegged. Then instruments were developed to sniff the fermentation and do the analysis.

The scent of fermenting beer—like the scent of a rose—is composed of evaporating molecules. It's these airborne molecules our nose converts into a smell. It's also these airborne molecules that headspace technology can capture, adding new pigments to the perfumer's palate.

What kinds of smells can be collected? How about the deep pungency of a box of Cuban cigars? Or the posh scent of the leather interior of a Mercedes Benz? Or the grassy smell of the third hole green at Pebble Beach? At Givaudan Roure, scientists, in search of the perfect leather note, once captured the scent of a horse barn. (It wasn't so much the horses, as the smell of leather saddles and harnesses they were after.) At Takasago, Kathleen Cameron tells me about a proposed scent that never made it to market based on the smell of freshly printed hundred-dollar bills. Call it the ultimate green note, predicated on the idea, no doubt, that nothing is more intoxicating than the smell of money.

"Do hundred-dollar bills smell different from, say, five-dollar bills?" I ask Cameron.

"Of course they do," she answers. "They smell richer."

Headspace technology involves vacuuming up molecules of the scent and running them through an instrument known as a gas chromatograph and mass spectrometer (GC/MS), which separates the fragrance into its chemical components and identifies them. Once the chemical blueprint is known, the scent can be reassembled by the organic chemist.

The technology is portable so that the scent of a rare flower found growing in a remote corner of the world can be captured without harming the flower. It's the ultimate in environmentally correct science. Instead of tearing up rare plants and shipping them off to be distilled—assuming you could find enough of a rare species to distill—fragrance scientists can literally pull the scent out of the air and duplicate it in a laboratory.

All you need to do is find the flower.

"We're looking for the 'tingle factor'," explains Tom McGee, as we rattle along a dirt road on the way to Irazú, a volcano more than 11,000 feet high in the middle of the Costa Rican rain forest. Irazú last erupted in 1963 and will hopefully stay quiet for now.

McGee, senior vice president of innovation and development for Givaudan Roure, has invited me on a scent trek, along with Ken Purzycki, Givaudan Roure's director of fragrance science, so I may see for myself the brave new world of fragrance chemistry.

Searching for new scents in the middle of the rain forest is one of the latest wrinkles in the high-stakes "what's new?" game of fragrance creation. "It's about catching the wave and staying ahead," McGee says. Givaudan Roure scientists have trekked off on a dozen such trips—to locales ranging from the Utah desert to the Malaysian jungle.

"We average about 10 to 25 new notes per trip, but maybe about half of them are good enough to hand over to the perfumers," he says.

Our guide on this trip is Bari Fernandez, an ecologist with the National Biodiversity Institute, a conservation organization engaged in a biological inventory of the Costa Rican rain forests. Costa Rica is an ideal hunting ground for such a scent trek, Purzycki explains, adding that there are more different flower species in 35 square miles of rain forest than in all of the United States. Surely we'll find something new to appease the Givaudan Roure perfumers back in Teaneck, New Jersey.

McGee instructs me in the truffle-hound approach to scent hunting. As we drive along I am supposed to poke my nose out the window of our Jeep, swivel my head around, and sniff. When things start to smell good we'll get out, start hiking, and sniff our way to the source of a promising smell. Look all around, McGee says. The next new scent might be above you (a flowering tree); in front of you (a flowering shrub); or beneath your foot (oops!). Don't just walk by a flower, he says. Experience it!

Why do flowers have fragrance, anyway? It's a matter of coevolution, explains McGee. To put it another way, it's matchmaking of the most intricate kind. Flowers are looking for insects to pollinate them. Their fragrance is a "come hither" signal to an insect, bird, or bat. If it's a flower that's bat-or fly-pollinated, the scent will usually mimic an animal smell. Flies feed on carrion, so the flower will use a rotten meat smell as a come-on. On the other hand, moth-or butterfly-pollinated flowers usually smell sweet, since sugar is the key to a nectar-loving insect's heart.

Scent hunting at night, McGee says, can be particularly rewarding. As a botanical rule of thumb, night-blooming flowers are more likely to have odor than day-blooming flowers. A pollinator like a moth, for example, relies strictly on fragrance to find its way to a flower at night. There are other guidelines for us to follow. White flowers have a higher probability of odor than brightly colored flowers. Above all, keep an open nose, McGee instructs. Let no

insect or leaf go unturned. A previous expedition yielded ants that when crushed gave off the scent of mint, bark that smelled of chocolate, and the smell of an isolated beach that ended up being used by the perfumers in Michael Jordan Cologne.

The cutting-edge technology is not perfect. Ken Purzycki, a veteran of half a dozen such expeditions, speaks remorsefully about the time he spent three hours on hands and knees studying a tiny marsh flower that smelled like lily of the valley. The equipment couldn't handle the moisture thrown off by the flower and shut down. Since the flower only blooms once a year Purzycki will have a long wait before he gets his next chance.

It's back in the Jeep and on the road again. Halfway down the blacktop that curls down from Irazú, Bari flags us to a stop. He leaps from the car, walks to the edge of the road where a tree is in flower, jumps up, and breaks off a stalk of tiny yellow flowers.

Ken sniffs the stalk and wrinkles his nose. "Fecal," he announces. "The perfumers would think I'd lost it if I brought that one back." Next, Tom and Ken confer over a rotten smelling leaf, decide it has sulfides, and agree that a flower that looks like Queen Anne's lace smells like plastic.

Ah, well. Finding beautiful new scents, like much else, is a matter of location, location, location. Tom says if we wind up with only one or two new scents we should consider ourselves successful. We'll try somewhere else. Along the way we stop again. This time Bari has spotted a jacaranda tree with delicate fern-like leaves and large, morning glory–like lavender flowers. We sniff. "Nothing," Ken says, dismissively. "Pretty to look at, but goes nowhere."

We might as well look around. So we troop single file down the shoulder of the road, noses twitching in anticipation.

"What about that small yellow one?" I ask, pointing to a buttercup-looking bloom close to the ground.

Everyone has a sniff. It's odorless. Zilch. We're still light years away from any tingle factor. The scent of consternation fills the air. But wait, Bari has found a shrub with a cluster of tiny yellow flowers that looks like a bouquet of

shooting stars. "Herbaceous, minty . . . ," Ken says, sniffing the spray. "Fresh, clean, bracing . . ." The adjectives roll out with ticker-tape rapidity. "Crisp, green, marigold-like . . ."

He holds the flower in front of my nose for my reaction.

"Yellow," I manage lamely. But it's not that different from any other minty, green smell already in the perfumer's bank of fragrances. We'll pass.

The next day we decide to try our luck searching for flowers in grassy lowlands. That's the beauty of Costa Rica's biological diversity. You can travel from rain forest to mangrove swamp in just hours. We head out from San Jose, and after an hour or so of driving up a dusty road that tapers to a thin lane of rock, we squeal to a halt along the fence line of a pasture. "Eau de cow," McGee says, sniffing the air as we start off on our trek. Along the way Purzycki pinches a bit of moss off a shrub. "Earthy, mushroomy," he opines, adding that every smell is potential fodder for perfumes. Meanwhile, Bari clambers up a tree to examine a fruit that looks like a huge green grenade. When split, the fruit turns out to smell like shelled peas.

Tingle factor, where are you? Theoretically, the odds should favor us. It's January, right after the rainy season, when flowers are supposed to pop. "It would be nice to find a flower with an original odor," Purzycki says wistfully, scanning foliage along the fence line.

He breaks the stem of a nearby shrub, sniffs it, then offers it to me with a smile. "Try this," he says. As I struggle to describe the familiar smell that will not become a word, he says, "Think Oscar Mayer." Instantly, the word for the smell forms on my tongue.

"It smells like baloney," I say.

Next we'll try the central highlands of Tapantí National Park. Along the way a whiff of perfume wafts into the car. Stop! I announce, and after backtracking along the road we discover the source of the fragrance: a shrub that grows out of a rocky cliff. The bush, covered in fist-sized sprays of delicate shell-pink flowers, probably belongs to the begonia family, according to Bari.

"Clean, slightly vanillic, Johnson's baby powder-like," Ken pronounces. That's the first good news of the day. The smell of baby powder is an olfactory American icon; it's one of those comfort notes beloved by the marketing gurus. We may come back the next day and take a headspace. But we'll continue on to Tapantí while we still have daylight.

The Tapantí trail is sopping wet. Even though January is supposed to be a dry month, we are not immune to the sudden appearance of a tropical downpour. The yearly rainfall here exceeds 250 inches. We slither along a sloppy trail, accompanied by the chatter of unseen birds and the slurping of mud against our boots. Bari stops to pluck a bug off a bush and rubs it. It releases a nasty, acrid smell and Bari flicks the bug away. Score: Bugs one; trekkers zero.

As we make our way down the trail a cloud of scent envelops us. The fragrance is a pleasant combination of sweet and spicy. It seems to be coming from a bush covered with tiny red flowers. Ken, the human thesaurus, goes to work. "Warm, jasmine, cinnamon . . . ," he says.

The scent is so diffusive you can smell it yards away. Meanwhile, the nebula of a distant memory is swirling in my mind. Red, I think. Fire engine red. Pepper. Hot. I mentally grope around, searching with the sort of I-know-it's-here-somewhere angst one reserves for a misplaced set of car keys.

I've got it. "Red hots!" I say. Ken nods in approval. The flowers really do smell like red hots. Darkness is falling and the trail looks too tricky to negotiate at night, so we agree to return the next day for the collection.

The next day we return to the park and set up the headspace collector, a unit that fits snugly into a metal briefcase and is light enough to be backpacked into remote jungle. Purzycki carefully positions a glass globe over a branch of

Tom McGee scrapes a bit of bark to elicit its smell during one of his Costa Rican expeditions. The result—a resinous odor similar to frankincense—piqued his interest. Fragrance scientists from major suppliers embark on several scent-seeking missions each year to destinations like Costa Rica, French Guiana, Malaysia, China, and Indonesia.

the flowers, tapes it in place, hooks up the plastic tubing, sets a series of dials, and starts filtering the scent through a tiny tube filled with beads made of an absorbant plastic known as Tenex. The beads will sponge up the molecules of fragrance from our small red jungle flower.

Before that happens we have to consider a more basic problem. When is the best time to collect the fragrance from this particular bloom? Flowers have their own rhythms, and each flower's fragrance will peak when its pollinators are likely to be around. Moth-pollinated flowers will be most fragrant at night; a rose, on the other hand, which is pollinated by bees, will start to peak in early morning when the insects are active. What are the settings on our jungle flower's biological clock?

Fortunately, the headspace collector takes samples on a 24-hour cycle; we won't have to baby-sit the flower to find out what time of day the scent is strongest. All we have to do is return for the harvest of molecules. Bari has tentatively identified our spicy-sweet flower as *Cavendishia quereme*. It's definitely a three-star tingle factor. In a small notebook Tom jots down: "Found at 17:45 hours, tubular white flowers with red bracts, white floral, undertone of spicy cinnamic notes." He hides the collection unit in the brush, turns on the unit, and tags the site with a strip of Day-Glo orange tape. The flower is nicknamed Bari 85 after our guide, and also because this is the 85th scent found by the Givaudan Roure scent trekkers in Costa Rica.

On the way back to San Jose we spot a hedge of pink-and-white trumpet-shaped flowers known locally as *reina de la noche*, or queen of the night. The scent is soft, citrusy, squeaky clean. There's a for-real tingle factor in this one—a slightly ticklish, ginger ale-like quality to the scent. "That's the citral you're smelling," Purzycki tells me, adding that it's a compound commonly found in lemon and lime oils. McGee and Purzycki are elated; they have been searching for this particular species for more than a year. By now it is too dark to do any more collecting. Bari will return to capture the scent another day.

"Hunting for new scents has opened a whole new world

of sense experience," Bari tells me that night at dinner. His dark eyes shine with excitement. "Before, in the jungle, I used to just listen for birds." He makes a series of *trills* and *clicks* to illustrate his point.

"But now . . . " He taps his sunburned nose.

Four weeks later, in the laboratory at Givaudan Roure headquarters in Teaneck, New Jersey, I inspect the gas chromatograph/mass spectrometer, or GC/MS. It's a gray metal box the size of an industrial microwave oven containing several hundred feet of hair-thin plastic tubing. This is the machine that will analyze the scents we've collected in Costa Rica. The tube of Tenex beads that has absorbed the molecules of fragrance from our tiny red jungle flower will be placed in the GC/MS and heated in gradual steps from 55 °C to 225 °C. At each temperature level different chemical elements boil off. Then the released molecules will be propelled through the tubing. Purzycki likens the process to shooing a gang of school boys through a tunnel. The small, agile ones—like citrus—wriggle out first; the big ones—like resins and musks—struggle through last. The molecules' progress through the tunnel of plastic tubing is clocked and the information converted to an EKG-like tracing that is the equivalent of a fragrance's heartbeat.

Each spike on the graph represents one chemical. The Bari 85 readout has about 200 spikes. Purzycki explains that of these only about 25 or so are relevant. Some of the elements, chemists know by experience, don't contribute anything to the smell and are discounted. "For example, a spike we ignore may represent a chemical that is related to solubility—it may allow the material to be dissolved in a liquid. But it contributes nothing to the fragrance itself."

His finger follows the tracing. "Here's citronellol," he says, pausing briefly. "Most roses have this chemical." He continues tracing the graph, then pauses again. "That big peak represents methyl salicylate, a key component in many fragrances." Methyl salicylate is found in oils like tuberose and spice wood.

The GC/MS measures chemical traces in parts per

Even a rotted piece of wood and the mushrooms growing on it are worth a closer inspection.
"We're interested in things that smell earthy and green," says Ken Purzycki. The combination of the
fungus and the moss growing on the branch emits a woody note.

trillion, and can, Purzycki tells me, pick out about 90 to 95 percent of the scent's components. As a last step a perfumer fine-tunes and balances the formula, comparing his memory of the scent with the readout in front of him. Since we didn't have a perfumer along on our trek, Purzycki's field notes will provide guidance. In the end, the human nose turns out to be indispensable.

It's taken the instruments a few hours to analyze the molecules of *Cavendishia quereme*. It's taken another two hours for the results to be interpreted, and yet a few hours more for the molecules to be reassembled by a chemist, and fine-tuned. I am now holding the bottle of Bari 85; I spray it in the air. It's 2,230 miles from the frozen February landscape of Teaneck, New Jersey, to the steaminess of the Costa Rican rain forest, yet a spritz of Bari 85 takes me back to the jungle in seconds.

As I breathe in the fragrance and contemplate the fine tracings on the graph that led to the re-creation of the scent of a jungle flower, I find myself wondering about a perfumer's feelings toward a machine that can take a scent, break it down, and punch out the formula in the course of an afternoon. Do perfumers feel envy when confronting such sophisticated technology? Do they feel threatened?

Most don't because GC/MS enhances a perfumer's insight. It enables a perfumer to see how a fragrance is chemically structured and allows him or her the *"Ah. So that's how that fragrance is put together!"* moment of understanding.

"It can't create a perfume," one perfumer told me. "But it is a learning tool. It's like picking someone's brain without them knowing you are doing it."

He tells me about the time he had diffusion problems, meaning his fragrances weren't sufficiently strong or lasting. So he asked to see the chemical profiles of Sophia Grojsman's fragrances, which are noted for their power and lushness. The perfumer figured that if he saw how they were constructed, he might learn something that would be helpful to his own work. It's like studying the paintings of the master artists. You would not want to copy their technique brushstroke for brushstroke, but the knowledge of how they worked can help inspire your own creativity.

But there's also a danger in GC/MS, particularly for young perfumers. As this perfumer says, "There is the risk that you'll end up doing nothing more than copying. You make your own version of Eternity or Allure. And you end up with soup."

Now that a GC/MS can pry open the formula of a scent, or at the very least give you a good idea of how it is put together, the safe-deposit box of secrecy would seem to be compromised. And it is. This is why there are so many knockoffs on the market, which appear in several guises. There's the outright counterfeit that may be packaged like and may even smell something like the original, but it's not. Says Sheila Hewett of Calvin Klein Cosmetics: "The cost of knockoffs is inestimable in customer goodwill. People will send back bottles of fragrances and complain; we'll look and find out it's counterfeit."

Then there's the copycat fragrance: the "if you like Eternity, you'll like Endless" product. Either way, it's an expensive thorn-in-the-side of the industry. The business of knockoffs has reportedly grown from a worth of 150 million dollars to a worth of 250 million dollars in five years. It's complicated by the fact that the name and package design of a perfume can be trademarked, but the formula cannot. How close are the knockoffs to the original? It depends. Like knockoffs of designer suits, some copies of fragrances use decent materials and are reasonably well constructed; others are pretty shabby. Neither are the real thing.

OPPOSITE Scott Mori climbs nearly 70 feet above the ground to examine the blooms of Guettarda spruceana, *a nocturnally flowering member of the coffee plant family. FOLLOWING PAGES Scents are captured from the wild with headspace technology, a technique in which scents are vacuumed through tubes filled with a material that absorbs scent molecules. Scientists analyze the molecules and construct a formula for the fragrance. To follow a flower's daily biorythm, its scent is collected in a different tube each hour.*

ABOVE *In the laboratory of the Instituto Nacional de Biodiversidad in Costa Rica, known as INBio, scientists attempt to classify unknown plants by comparing the leaf structures to those of known species. Learning the family to which a new fragrant plant belongs helps fragrance scientists, who can investigate other members of that family for similar smells.* FOLLOWING PAGES *In pursuit of the ethereal—an orchid's scent— Braja Mookherjee, a scientist at IFF, uses a glass-fiber needle capable of absorbing fragrance molecules. The needle is coated with a liquid that absorbs the molecules so they can be analyzed and replicated synthetically.*

"Gas chromatography and mass spectrometry seems to have turned formulas into an open book," I say to Tom McGee, during the course of a phone conversation. "Are there any secrets left in the industry?"

He sighs. "Not many."

There is at least one secret left, however—captive materials. Captives are aroma chemicals developed by a supplier, such as damascenone, a synthetic rose created by Firmenich in the 1970s, or sandalore, a synthetic sandalwood. Nearly all of the big suppliers have research programs devoted to the search for new materials. When a new synthetic is created the supplier patents it.

Captives, which are the exclusive property of a supplier for the 17-year-long life of the patent, are often the special ingredient, the extra little something, that can help lift a perfume from good to great, or make it stand out from the pack. It's also one of the reasons that a GC/MS can only duplicate an existing formula, up to a point.

An example is the synthetic floral note, hedione, created by Firmenich, and first used in a major commercial perfume by Edmond Roudnitska when he composed Eau Sauvage in 1966. "We broke our noses to find out what was in Eau Sauvage," a French perfumer from Givaudan Roure told me. "It makes that fragrance dance." You can analyze any new fragrance through GC/MS, of course, and you'll know at once that something new is being used, but if the new material is a captive, isolating it can take years. For 17 years the supplier has an edge over its rivals. A few years before the patent on a new material runs out, a supplier may offer it for sale to other suppliers, but once the patent expires it's a free-for-all, and anyone can play with the new chemical.

What's it like for a perfumer to get a new molecule to play with? "There's a huge learning curve in the beginning," says Kari Arienti, a perfumer with Givaudan Roure. "But once you hit it off with a new chemical, it's a massive love affair. It's like having a new piece of jewelry you want to wear all the time. We have a new cassis base that has a green note—it was introduced a few years ago—and I've been using it in just about everything."

Getting a new chemical to work with is like Christmas, says Thierry Wasser, a perfumer at Firmenich. "Sometimes you say, 'Wow! A huge fire truck. I'm going to run around and make lots of noise with it and drive everyone crazy.' But sometimes you don't even know what it is or what to do with it."

"It's a pretty note, an interesting note," James Bell, a senior perfumer at Givaudan Roure, tells me. I've just sprayed a little Bari 85 on a blotter and handed it to him. When I remark that Bari 85 reminds me of Pepsodent toothpaste, with a hint of wintergreen Life Savers thrown in, Bell explains that the minty smell is due to the high level of methyl salicylates. "Anyway, it's not a finished fragrance," he says. "You'd want to round it off with other notes before you could do anything with it." He is working on a high-end perfume, and, handing me a blotter dipped into his work-in-progress, asks if I'd like to have a sneak preview.

"How do you like it?" he wants to know. When I say that the thickly floral fragrance invokes a vase of hyacinths on a mahogany table in the middle of a Victorian parlor hung with dark, velvet curtains, his face falls.

"That's not what I'm looking for," he says. "I need to brighten it, make it more contemporary. I'll add muguet and cyclamen to give it a lighter, more watery texture."

"It must be daunting to have so many notes to choose from," I remark.

"Two thousand, three hundred to be exact," he replies.

"And now you'll have another one," I say, reminding him of the newly discovered Bari 85.

"Wonderful!" he responds. "Even 2,300 is never enough."

SIX

Promise Her Anything

The battle to hook the customer climaxes at the counter. "A customer must fall into a fragrance immediately," Yves de Chiris of Quest says. "Any hesitation and you lose."

There's a lot to lose. The cosmetics and fragrance department in any department store is a mother lode of revenue. In 1997, at Saks Fifth Avenue in New York, cosmetics added up to nearly a fifth of the store's 420 million dollars in revenues according to the *New York Times*. It's a question of volume. A fur coat costs a lot more than a bottle of fragrance, but there are many more bottles of fragrance sold than fur coats.

I visit Sephora, a store devoted to fragrance, located on the Champs-Élysées in Paris. Even at nine at night, Sephora, which stays open until midnight, is packed wall-to-wall with people. They're young, stylish, and having a good time. Sephora is the MTV of perfume stores; it's retailing as theater. The decor is space station-modern with glass, chrome, and polished granite floors. Fragrances are displayed as objets d'art. An electronic ticker tape at one end of the store flashes the price of Chanel No. 5 or cK One in New York, Buenos Aires, and London. Salespeople dress head-to-toe in black. Even the pens they hand you to sign

your credit card sales slip are black and sleek. It's all so chic. It's all so hip. It's to die for.

I am intoxicated by the sight and smell of so much fragrance. Please look at me, touch me, and, most of all, smell me, the displays scream. I accept the invitation and spritz my way through the alphabetically arranged shelves, from Angel to Zino.

Les Belles de Nina Ricci in its Day-Glo green and fuchsia bottle has as its dominant note an unlikely tomato leaf scent. It smells astringent, livid, chartreuse green. Angel, by Thierry Mugler, smells sticky, sweet, like a fairground after closing. It is a bold, polarizing fragrance that women either love or hate. Is it my imagination or does Yves Saint Laurent's Champagne, recently renamed Yvresse because the champagne growers of France protested appropriation of the name and dragged the designer through the courts, have the ticklish effervescence of champagne? Yes, affirms perfumer Sophia Grojsman of IFF, who worked on it. The sparkle lies in the top notes—nectarine, lychee, and blue rose (an imaginary rose that does not exist anywhere except in the perfumer's palate).

These and hundreds more sit on shelves at Sephora,

Perfume is an ephemeral yet beautiful accessory for Allee Bennett, preparing for the evening in Austin, Texas. Like many women, she wears a favorite fragrance on all occasions, and often carries a small bottle for refreshing the scent during the day.

yet they're just a fraction of the thousand or more brands on the market worldwide. With more, many more, to come. The industry is in a hamster-wheel bind. More than a hundred perfumes were launched in the United States last year. "The industry has become like a bike that can only stand up if it keeps moving," Olwen Wolfe, a Paris-based consultant, tells me.

"It's a 'what's new' business," affirms Ann Gottlieb, the New York consultant. "I call them the BIC fragrances. It's the disposable era. Perfume has gone from an elixir that helps define you, to an accessory like a throwaway pair of stockings. This is a generation with a very short attention span."

The quest for the classic perfume—one that's been around for ten, twenty, or more years and is passed down from generation to generation—has, for the most part, evaporated. These days the winning formula is hit fast, hit big, move on. Two decades ago scents took one, two, even three years to develop. Now they're produced in weeks. They also drop like flies. Of ten launches maybe two will break even, seven will fold, one might succeed. The creation and launching of a fragrance is a costly roll of the dice. A company can spend 20 million dollars or more to introduce a new scent that can quickly flop.

Why take the risk?

For the money, of course. For mountains of money. Take Calvin Klein's cK One, the benchmark blockbuster of the 1990s. That fragrance shipped out more than 250 million dollars' worth in 1996. Or consider a classic like Chanel No. 5, which, according to consultant Allan Mottus, has turned out more than a billion dollars in sales over the last 75 years. ("We have?" responded a Chanel executive, when asked for verification. "We don't discuss figures. We're not about that.")

Still, even a top-tier company like Chanel can miss the boat. There is no sure ticket to success. "Ever have a flop?" I asked Susan Duffy, executive director of public relations for fragrance and beauté at Chanel in New York.

"Once. A *disappointment*," she said carefully. "Egoïste. A men's fragrance. It was too sophisticated and subtle. Also, the name was a turn-off."

If the upside is spectacular, the downside is scary. Not only can you lose your shirt, Allan Mottus cautions, you can bring a whole company down. One corpse left by the wayside, the *Financial Times of London* reported, was the 40 million dollars lost by the French luxury goods conglomerate LVMH Moët Hennessy Louis Vuitton on Christian Lacroix's aptly named C'est la Vie in 1989. Another sinking ship was Clandestine by Guy Laroche, which folded after six months. Some fragrances get killed in the early stages of development and never even get on the shelf.

Celebrity fragrances have a particularly high casualty rate. A big name can carry a fragrance only so far, and often not far enough. Perfumes by Cher, Sophia Loren, Joan Collins, Pelé, and Michael Jackson have failed. The indefatigable Elizabeth Taylor, who has even appeared on the Internet to pitch her fragrance Passion, is the most notable exception, but even she misses. Passion and White Diamonds sell well; Black Pearls apparently does not.

Kermit the Frog put his webbed imprimatur on a fragrance: Amphibia, a citrus-scented blue liquid with "green" notes. Christmas sales in 1995 were brisk, but it lasted only a year. Can Barbie, Ken's beloved, beat the odds? Her fragrance is on the market now. It is pretty, sweet, and packaged in bubblegum-pink.

Then there was Armani's Giò, a multimillion-dollar fizzle launched in 1993.

What went wrong?

It certainly wasn't the launch party. *Tout* New York and Hollywood showed up. Superlatives flowed as easily as the wine. "The party of the year, if not the decade," crowed *Harper's Bazaar.*

Guests crowded a Manhattan office building basement reconstituted as a Moroccan palace. Whoopi Goldberg, Cher, and Geena Davis smiled for the cameras; a stoney-faced Dustin Hoffman did not. Lee Radziwill wore Armani; Joan Rivers did not. They all ate from imported Moroccan brass dinnerware under 10,000 square feet of muslin that was nipped and tucked into a tent. They sipped mint tea and champagne and nibbled on caviar and candied

ABOVE *The promise of Allure, a fragrance launched by Chanel in 1996, is captured for a new advertising campaign by photographer Herb Ritts. The ad campaign includes a variety of up-and-coming models rather than a single superstar, to suggest that every woman has her own allure.* FOLLOWING PAGES *Impeccably styled drinks in coordinated colors add to the atmosphere at the launch party for Flirt, a new fragrance from Prescriptives. Slender glasses of champagne, seltzer, and punch tinted lavender to match Flirt's packaging, frame a bottle of the Chardonnay-colored perfume. No detail escapes attention at launch parties. The fragrance features ginger notes—so does the punch.*

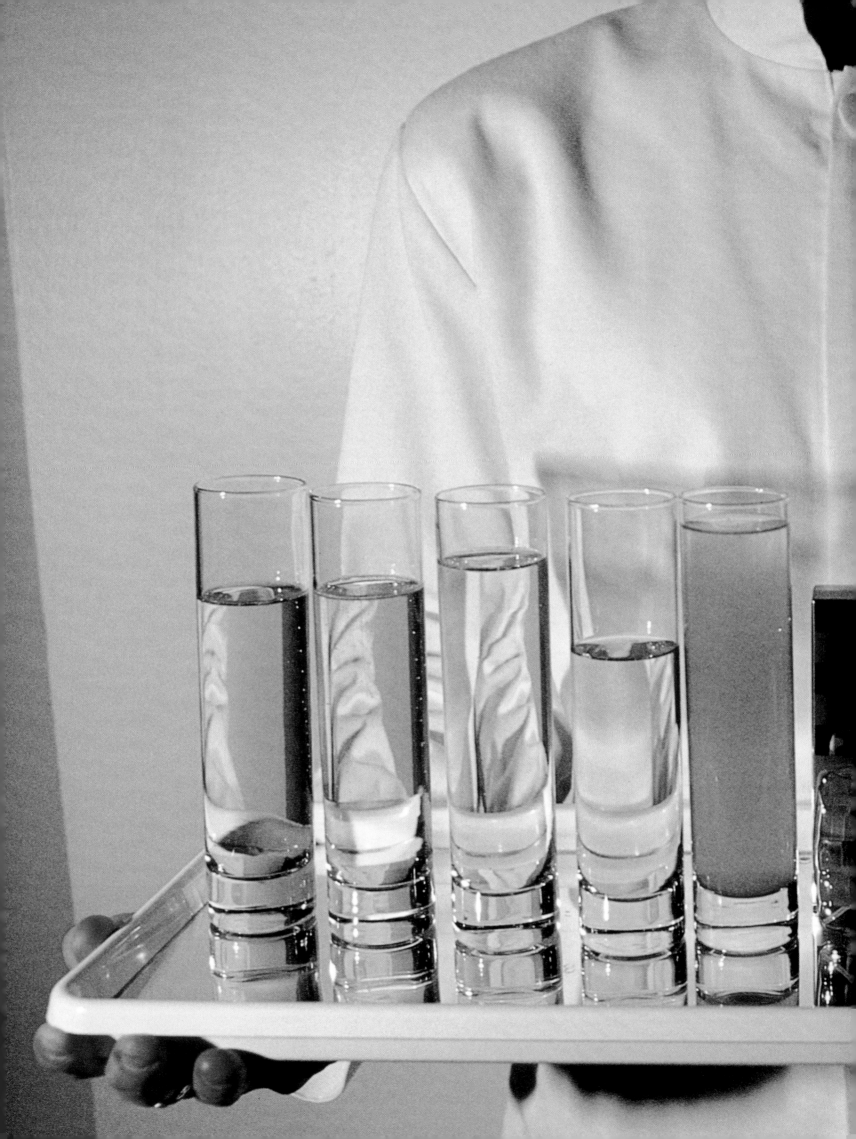

ABOVE Jungk—an Asian all-girl rock band—performs at the "East Meets West" Flirt launch in New York City. The face of Flirt is Jungk's lead singer, Ling, a Malaysian model and kung fu expert, who will appear in ads for the perfume. FOLLOWING PAGES For a modern fragrance adventure, visit Sephora, the state-of-the-art perfume store on the Champs-Élysées in Paris. Shoppers undergo a complete sensory experience—they admire the display of bottles, smell the perfumes, and hear the beauty commercials that blast from massive video monitors.

kumquats in the shade of palm trees flown in for the occasion. The party had been carefully choreographed by Robert Isabell, the David Merrick of New York party planners, who'd flown to Milan twice to discuss details with Giorgio Armani himself. The cost for the big night added up to nearly a million dollars.

And all that money couldn't buy a hit fragrance?

"As much as we try to be analytic, as much as we study the trends and market test, at the end of the day it's a crapshoot," says one director of marketing. Against odds, companies throw the dice. Snake eyes today; perhaps seven on the first roll tomorrow. Two years after the Giò bust, Armani introduced Acqua di Giò. It does very well.

Does the world *really* need a new fragrance?

"Yes," says Leonard Lauder, chairman and CEO of the Estée Lauder Companies. "Tastes change."

"Yes," says Patrick Firmenich, vice president of Firmenich, "I think the world needs a new fragrance as much as it needs a new sculpture or painting."

"Certainly not," says Véra Strübi, president of Thierry Mugler Parfums. "Unless it can be creative and different."

Bob Aliano is hoping that PF1, short for Prestige Fragrance #1, will be creative and different. "It's the battle of the Titans," he tells me.

A big, affable man with a shiny helmet of black hair and a toothbrush-like mustache, Aliano, vice president of creative perfumery worldwide for Giorgio Beverly Hills, explains that project PF1 has come down to a run-off between Firmenich and IFF. Suppliers like IFF and Firmenich may spend a quarter of a million dollars to create a fragrance like PF1 on spec, with no guarantee they'll win the contract to supply the "juice," as the scent is known.

IFF, where I now am with Aliano, is gambling on a fragrance submission based on a sundust orchid note. The orchid, a small, rare, golden yellow orchid that grows in tropical Asia, has been synthetically re-created in the lab. Across town Firmenich has its money on a fragrance based on a merlot note.

Aliano explains his concept for PF1: "A perfume so beautiful men will miss you when you leave the room. To sell for $300 an ounce. Maybe more. The sky's the limit!"

Braja Mookherjee, IFF's vice president and director of natural product research, enters and announces that several new molecules have been found in the orchid note.

New molecules! Aliano perks up. He's like the kid who has just found the long-coveted, shiny, red-and-chrome bicycle under the Christmas tree. "That's the story," he enthuses. "Never before smelled by humans." The words tumble out nonstop. He is speaking in exclamation points. "We took nothing away from nature but the air! You'll never be able to smell anything like this in your lifetime!"

Sophia Grojsman, the perfumer on the project, sprays a bunch of blotter cards with different submissions and passes them out. "Number two is muted. Six opens to musk. Seven adds coconut." She sniffs the blotter. "Maybe a little too much coconut."

Aliano likes number five, a pretty floral. All heads nod energetically.

"I want it bigger, bolder," he says. "I want to make a statement that this is the best. It breaks all the rules. It's PERFECT! In fact," he adds, half to himself, "Perfect may become the name."

Three months later I call Aliano to check on the status of PF1.

"He's no longer here," a secretary says. "He left ten days ago."

I track him down. "I took a golden parachute," he says wearily by phone from California. "I'm sort of tired of this whole industry. Not the creative part," he quickly adds. "It's the strictly numbers attitude. The testing a thing to death. The layers and layers of people. PF1 just wasn't going to happen. I hear they've canceled the project."

Six months later I make a final check-up call to Bob Aliano. He tells me he's on the verge of jumping back into the fragrance business. He's buzzing with the possibility of big deals, his enthusiasm once again uncontainable. He's itching to take the plunge. "I'm going to give the consumer

Visitors compare notes at Sephora's perfume organ—the traditional instrument of perfumers. An employee equipped with blotters stands behind the array of bottles and conducts customers through a sampling of individual ingredients and finished fragrances. Some will buy, but for others simply touring the ultrachic, approximately 16,000-square-foot superstore is enjoyment enough.

value that's so unprecedented," he says. The company he's putting together will consist of himself, a partner to handle the corporate/financial end of things, and an office manager. That's it, he says. It will be a low-overhead operation with no big corporate structure, no endless meetings, and no large-scale testing.

Marketing first, then fragrance. It is usual these days for the bottle, the name, and the advertising campaign of a new scent to be developed well in advance of the fragrance itself. As the push for marketing picks up speed, the attention paid to the "juice" itself seems to get left behind.

"The amount of money companies put into fragrance itself is half of what it was say, ten years ago," says Roger Schmid, president of fragrances and cosmetics for Dragoco, a German-based supplier. "I'm not saying the package isn't important," he adds. "But maybe if you want to sell something for a bit longer, you should put something inside it. It's easier to understand packaging than fragrance. Suppose you come to the fragrance industry from a background in selling cereals. You are used to developing the externals. It's like running a restaurant and taking tremendous care about the linen and tableware, while totally ignoring the chef in the kitchen." The best fragrances, he adds, citing perfumes by Chanel and Estée Lauder as examples, often come in the simplest packages.

"This is craft, not art," perfumer Annie Buzantian says pragmatically when I ask if the market-driven nature of the business bothers her.

"The days past were like Nirvana for a creative person," sighs Karyn Khoury, vice president of corporate fragrance development worldwide for the Estée Lauder Companies. "It was art for art's sake: Wonderful while it lasted, but it couldn't exist forever. Most of us understand and have adapted. Yes, there is a lot of razzmatazz associated with the selling of fragrance. Unfortunately, it's how you get the product in front of the customer. We still believe that in the end the thing that matters is the beauty of what's in the bottle."

But razzmatazz rules. It is the siren song of advertising that leads us to the counter.

In 1996 the industry spent 417 million dollars to trumpet the product on television, in print, and everywhere from bus-stop placards to billboards to popcorn bags. In the never-never land of perfume advertising, the dogs (they always seem to be golden retrievers) never have fleas; dirty laundry doesn't pile up; the grass never needs cutting; and there are no pimples or bad hair days. Even the beads of perspiration on the finely muscled torsos look as if they smell not of sweat but of the scent being pitched.

"The industry is great at making a personal hygiene product into a bellwether of civilization," says a journalist for the fashion press. We were at an industry breakfast, standing by a table cloaked in white linen and set with pitchers of fresh orange juice, silver trays of tiny croissants, and artfully arranged slices of kiwi, melon, pineapple, papaya, and strawberries.

"Well, after all, it is the fashion business," I say philosophically as legions of women in black air-kiss their way around the room.

Surely the genius of sell is Calvin Klein. Consider the ads for Obsession: a tangle of bodies (two men, one woman . . . or was it the other way around?). "Repulsive," says a competitor. "But they stick with you. We spent seven million dollars in advertising our product, and women in a focus group said they'd never heard of it."

The Calvin Klein fragrance empire reigns on the 22nd floor of Trump Tower in New York City. In the blindingly beige decor of beige walls and beige rugs, with a white orchid as accent on a blond wood desk, nearly everyone wears black. I talk to Sheila Hewett, vice president of marketing and advertising for Calvin Klein Cosmetics.

"The hardest thing is to take something people don't need and make it part of their lives," she explains. "How do you get their attention? You scream loud. You read trends. You look at what's happening in the world. Minimalism is coming out of London; we go to London."

Take the Generation Xers, the target market for cK One

and cK Be. The target group—20- to 32-year-olds—grew up in a world of changing relationships, ethnic diversity, and gender blurring. This is a group looking to define itself. "They're wearing fragrance to be part of the group," says Hewett. "They're from divorced families, so friends become more important. There are no rules. It's assimilating to an attitude."

To sell to this group, Hewett explains, "you watch a movie like *Beavis and Butthead Do America* and wonder where it will be in 18 months. You ask what are they reading, what are they driving? It's anthropology. You create what they want almost before they know they want it.

"Once upon a time, you want jasmine, you buy Shalimar. Now fragrances have to have a story line, and you have to boil it down to a sentence. Obsession is the dark side of us all. The fantasy that maybe you don't want to talk about, but you know is there. Escape is wanting to get away from it all. Eternity is about a relationship or family or commitment. cK One is about sharing. With cK Be you're an individual before you're part of a group."

Calvin Klein's trump is his over-the-horizon radar. He senses when the consumer is ready to cuddle up at home under a taupe cashmere blanket, revisit Camelot, and be doused in Eternity. He knows when the time is ripe for a unisex fragrance like cK One.

Calvin Klein can hear the grass growing, a public relations woman in the industry says admiringly. "He's edgy, ahead of the curve, and," she adds with awe, "he never goes over the line."

One might say "almost never." When cK One and cK Be were launched the ads featured a lineup of scrawny, pale, tattooed kids, one with—could it be?—the faint tracks of a user. Was the hint of "heroin chic" used to sell the fragrance?

"Sure, there was lots of suggestion," Sheila Hewett says. "But they were not track marks. It was a scar on the model from an accident.

"Is Calvin Klein's advertising too controversial because it's Calvin Klein, or is it too controversial because you've got to be controversial to cut through today?" Hewett muses. "I'll go to dinner parties and sit there and listen to heated arguments about the cK Be or cK One advertisements, and when they're finished I'll say, 'I am thrilled. You sat here for 10 or 15 minutes and went on nonstop, which means you know my ads intimately. So they're obviously a big success. It doesn't mean you have to like them.'"

Still, a tincture of nostalgia lingers among some for understated suggestion instead of in-your-face shocking. "They don't make them like they used to," laments Fernando Aleu, chairman of Compar, which produces perfumes by Paco Rabanne and Carolina Herrera. We are lunching at Le Chantilly in New York, and Aleu, silver haired-handsome in a Fernando Lamas way, shifts the conversation to the subject of fragrance advertising and the taglines that have become Madison Avenue mantras of our era.

"With Norell," Aleu intones, affecting a smoky Bacall-like voice, "each time is like the first time."

"Promise her anything, but give her Arpège," I counter.

"Paco Rabanne will make you remember," he says. "What is remembered is up to you."

"Every women alive wants Chanel No. 5," I reply.

"We don't have good ads anymore," Aleu laments. "People got hung up with nudity and sex."

He cites the ad for Tabu. The violinist passionately embraces his pianist. He has pulled her to him; she is half out of her chair. He encircles her waist with one hand and holds his violin aloft with the other. Her head is thrown back to receive his kiss; one hand rests helplessly on the piano.

The ad, introduced to American readers in 1941, launched "the longest commercial kiss in history," the *New York Times* said. It is a bodice-ripper scene, full of flushed cheeks, heaving chests, swooning melodrama. And it worked. For years, mail addressed simply "Tabu violinist, New York" reached the company. That ad last ran in the early 1980s. A new version of the ad plays off the old in a campy parody in which the roles are reversed and a woman painter is impulsively grabbed and kissed by her male model.

TABU

The Forbidden Fragrance by *Dana*

LEFT Sold with a kiss, Tabu's memorable advertisement has helped keep it in the fragrance game since its 1931 launch. The now-famous scene was painted by René Prinet in 1898 and originally titled "The Kreutzer Sonata." ABOVE A contemporary variation still gets the point across.

"I'd rather have one moment of uncontrollable attraction than 20 naked people," Aleu reflects. "Perfume can make you run away from or to something. Our industry is based on the simple fact of attraction. It can be the power of a memory, a simple pleasure, or sex."

The killer lure is the scented strip. Open any fashion magazine, find the fragrance ad, pull open the tab or flap, and you get a whiff of the newest scent on the market.

The old scratch-and-sniff technology depended on micro-encapsulated droplets of oil that were released when you ran a nail across a strip. Unfortunately, the oil could and sometimes did leak, scenting a whole magazine. In the fall of 1992, after readers complained, the *New Yorker* refused to run the strips. Two years later, after the technology improved, they were back.

Today's state-of-the-art strips are put out by Arcade, the leading fragrance sampling company, with headquarters in Chattanooga, Tennessee. Their seals feature a dab of fragrance in a leak-proof tiny foil packet, or a small disc-shaped plastic seal that peels off to reveal the fragrance beneath.

"The industry once used glass vials with samples of perfume," explains Roger Barnett, Arcade's president and CEO. "If you smiled, you got a handful and never had to buy the fragrance—and they were expensive to produce."

The scented strip carried the advertising message to the customer's home, preempting the need for a store visit. The tryst between customer and fragrance could take place in one's living room. It was convenient, private, and because the amount of the sample was so small, it didn't cannibalize sales.

Today, Arcade turns out more than a billion scented strips a year. A company like Calvin Klein Cosmetics will,

A hands-on entrepreneur with a nose for what women wanted, Estée Lauder helped put the American fragrance
industry on the map beginning with her 1953 hit, Youth Dew. She sold women on her perfumes—and they are still
buying. "Different moods require different scents," she used to say, according to her daughter-in-law, Evelyn.
"You don't wear the same shoes every day—why wear the same scent?"

in the course of a new launch, send out a barrage of 40 million or so at a cost of millions of dollars. "Fragrance is one of the few consumer products you can't put in words," Barnett says. "No one will buy without sampling first."

What makes a winning fragrance?

"Good juice, good name, good marketing, good advertising, good packaging," Sheila Hewett of Calvin Klein says, ticking them off on her fingers as we sit in her office.

And the most difficult part?

"The name, the name, the name."

It's torture because of trademark clearance, she says. It is one of the ironies of the fragrance business that the formula for a fragrance cannot be patented or copyrighted, but a name can be trademarked. The process of coming up with something original and then making sure you have clear claim, not just in this country but everywhere in the world, is a logistical nightmare.

"It's like going to the motor vehicle bureau in every country around the world," says Hewett. "Like trying to get the post office to do something at top speed. It's impossible. You have to do it in every single market around the world you want to be in. And the trademark offices in each are all different, all archaic, all paper-pushing."

Bob Aliano, while still at Giorgio Beverly Hills, remembers the hunt for the name of a new fragrance ultimately called Red.

He recalls a meeting with the creative agency assigned to the account and sitting through an hour of buildup and wait'll-you-see-this fanfare. The hype was on. Finally, the account executive flipped the page to reveal the knock-'em-dead name: "Privacy."

Silence shrouded the room.

"I know the people at Modess," Aliano said. "It would make a great name for a sanitary napkin."

Aliano ultimately decided to call the fragrance Red. "It's strong, powerful, a beautiful name," he explained. "And from a design point of view, it's only three letters. You can make the lettering on the package big and bold." Much hand-wringing followed as the connotations of that word were bandied around the conference table. *Red? Road kill, communists, blood, guts. . . .* Aliano soothed that bout of anxiety, only to run up against another small detail: A trademark search revealed that the name was already owned by the American designer Geoffrey Beene. But that fragrance had faded from the market and was no longer on the shelves. Might Beene be willing to sell the name? Aliano asked.

"Geoffrey says he will never, ever part with it," Beene's representative said.

Aliano named a price. The representative countered. And so it went until Aliano bought the name for $65,000. The fragrance, Giorgio's Red, introduced in 1989, went on to sell 94 million dollars' worth its first year out.

Sometimes the sale doesn't happen. Contradiction, launched by Calvin Klein Cosmetics in the fall of 1997, was going to be called Intuition until the Klein company learned that the name "Intuition" was already owned by the Aveda Corporation, the Minneapolis-based beauty products company that uses only plant-derived ingredients.

"The Calvin Klein company offered me a million dollars," Horst Rechelbacher, Aveda's founder and chair told me. "And, they said, 'You can still use the name.'"

He refused the offer.

"A million dollars is a lot of money," I mused to Rechelbacher.

He waved his hand dismissively. "I want my independence. They use synthetics in their perfumes. Mine are natural."

Back at Calvin Klein Cosmetics I hear another chapter to the story.

The company offered a million dollars for the name, says a Calvin Klein executive, and Rechelbacher did turn it down. The executive told him to think about it. The executive reported, "Later we got a letter from his lawyer saying we could have the name for 10 million dollars.

"We said, 'Forget it.'"

Fernando Aleu of Compar, which distributes Calandre

by Paco Rabanne, recalls his first meeting with Diana Vreeland, the legendary editor of *Vogue*, who promptly launched into a rat-a-tat-tat monologue on the attributes of the name Calandre.

"Don't you think that Calandre is a divine name for a fragrance," she said to Aleu. "So ridiculously clever. It does mean the grill of a car, doesn't it? Just think about it. A husband loving his wife and asking her, 'What are you wearing, dear?' 'I am wearing the grill of a car!' I love it. Perfume names are usually so corny. This is not; this is bizarre and there is nothing wrong with being bizarre. But corny, ah, *mon Dieu!*"

One day in 1946, a tiny plane buzzed by the Place du Trocadéro in Paris and released an armada of small green-and-white parachutes, a tiny bottle of Ma Griffe suspended beneath each. A new fragrance had been launched—literally.

If all it took were a small plane these days. . . .

"The first advice I got from Mrs. Estée Lauder was that I should buy the salesgirls a box of candy. I wish I could get away with even a box of Godiva chocolates today," her son, Leonard Lauder, CEO of the Estée Lauder Companies, says wistfully. "It costs me 15 to 20 million dollars to launch today."

As the ante gets bigger, to test or not to test has become the question. Testing means putting your fragrance in front of a consumer panel for evaluation while it is in development. Testing also means putting together a focus group: a marketing study in which a group of people are put in a room and asked a series of questions by a moderator to determine their preferences, habits, and attitudes as consumers. The ultimate purpose is to see if your fragrance concept will fit your targeted audience.

Testing is a controversial topic in the industry. There are those who maintain a cutting edge fragrance will never make it to market if tested. Innovative, avant-garde doesn't test well, the argument goes; people only give good marks to the familiar and blandness results.

The pro-testing contingent says that if you're going to put 20 million dollars on the line, you've got to make very sure people are going to like it. A company can't afford to take that kind of risk when so much money is at stake.

Christian Dior Parfums prefers not to leave anything to chance. It tests a new product three times, according to Patrick Choël, president of the company. The concept of a new fragrance gets tested, the suppliers test their submissions, and there's a final test of the finished scent.

Angel, radically new when introduced in 1992 because of its combined notes of chocolate, caramel, and patchouli, wasn't tested at all. "We knew it would never do well if tested," Véra Strübi, president of Thierry Mugler Parfums, says. It was a risky go-by-the-gut move and it paid off. Angel went to the top of the charts in France and sells very well in high-end specialty stores in this country.

"'Who needs testing?' my mother used to say," Leonard Lauder recalls. "She'd be horrified at the amount of money we spend. The world has changed so dramatically." His mother, Estée Lauder, now in her nineties and no longer active in the company she created, was a go-with-your-gut-instinct street fighter with the motivational force of a bulldozer. Mrs. Lauder helped jump-start the American fragrance industry with pivotal big-hit scents like Youth Dew and, later, White Linen and Beautiful. Youth Dew, introduced in 1953, was a phenomenon. Originally a bath oil, it was molasses-brown, with an unheard of concentration of more than 40 percent oil. Recalls her daughter-in-law, Evelyn Lauder, a senior corporate vice president of the company, "Everyone said, 'You can't sell a dark brown perfume.' She said, 'Watch me.'"

In the early years Estée Lauder was the company. A one-woman show—she did her own fragrance development and marketing and oversaw package design. She'd materialize unannounced for a white-glove inspection at the counter where her products were sold, then instruct salesgirls on how to sell. "Put a dab of fragrance on the back of your customer's right hand," she'd tell them, explaining that later the customer would brush her hair, catch a whiff of scent, and return to buy.

Selling was her joy. In New York, during the seventies, she'd lunch at Orsini's when it was the place to be seen. She'd make an entrance, sit down magisterially, then table-hop between courses. She'd be wearing royal blue or bottle green to match her eyes, and always a matching hat, and gloves. She'd pull a flacon from her handbag and spray wrists left and right with her newest creation. Protest was useless; there was no saying "no."

She was self-made and shrewd, controlling and intense, captivated by details and absolutely brilliant. She could provoke an employee to tears, then feed them chicken soup. She'd visit her daughter-in-law, Evelyn, and move the furniture around. She'd go to IFF to check on the perfumers who worked on her fragrances. The call would come at the last minute: "Mrs. Lauder is on the way." The perfumers would say, "Oh, my God," and scurry down the block to have their shoes polished. She could be dif-ficult; she had that dark complexity that goes with fierce drive. "Yes, but you understand and you love her for it," Evelyn Lauder says. She'd spend three days on a train going from New York to Dallas to sell to some depart-ment store buyer. Who knew from marketing depart-ments? She knew what women wanted and how to sell to them. She invented "gift with purchase": Buy a bottle of fragrance and you'd get a free lipstick. In the days when feminism was a wisp of an idea, she told women they didn't have to wait for their husband or boyfriend to give them perfume. They could buy it themselves.

Like her older contemporaries, Charles Revson and Helena Rubenstein, Estée Lauder was a giant in the Amer-ican business of beauty. She loved the big statement. She didn't enter, she swept into a room. She wore stylish, massive, gold jewelry. Her office was like French patisserie—acres of silk braid and tassels, an oyster-white silk couch, powder-blue velvet curtains, and an ormolu cabinet full of decorative objects. "She didn't know from subtle," says an employee. "How much I miss her." She was bigger than life, and so were her perfumes.

That was then; this is now. During the years when Estée Lauder was running the company, you could afford to wait five to seven years for a fragrance to hit its stride, points out Karyn Khoury of the Estée Lauder Companies.

Lauder's fragrance Beautiful, for example, took about five years to reach bestseller status. Now, ideally, you'd like it to peak and hit the top five right away. Estée Lauder would be horrified. Testing can run into the tens of thousands of dollars per panel or consumer group. Some of the larger multinationals probably spend millions of dollars to test in the course of a year. Like everything else in the fragrance business, testing is not a sure thing. It can't predict a huge hit, but it can, advocates say, provide a measure of insur-ance against a huge flop. With the launch of Pleasures in 1995, the Lauder companies began big-scale market-testing of some of their new products—but only as one piece of the decision-making process.

"Mrs. Lauder didn't believe in large-scale testing," Khoury remembers, adding that at the most, she'd tolerate a small in-house panel. "We'd go to 30 or 40 girls in the office with a new fragrance and say 'What do you think?' As long as she was running things that was it. If the results didn't agree with what she thought, she'd say, 'What do they know?' And she was right. She'd test her fragrances on cab drivers; she'd test the ladies she lunched with; she'd test the women she played mah-jongg with; she'd test her maid. I used to call them the grandmother tests. They could drive you crazy. But she had consummate faith in her own instincts. She had vision. And you can never have vision by committee."

FOLLOWING PAGES Parisian pet stylist Marie Cavalieri D'Oro pampers her Yorkshire terrier, Pacha, with a misting of vanilla-scented Chien Chic de Paris, a fragrance especially formulated for dogs. D'Oro operates an upscale canine and feline salon in Paris, where she regularly spritzes her animal clients with scent following their shampoos and trims.

What's hot? What's not? Fashion is perishable, allowing for a seasonal revolution in colors, cut, and fabric. The fashion of fragrance, too, changes in a blink, veering from simple, clean, fresh to lush, heavy, exotic, and back again. "Fashion dies very young, so we must forgive it everything," said French playwright Jean Cocteau.

What makes miniskirts go out of style and lush, heavy perfumes come in? It's a conjunction of the stars and of social, economic, and cultural forces. The Reagan feel-good years of the eighties were loud and big and bright, and so were perfumes like Giorgio and Obsession. People were putting potent substances up their noses; on their bodies they splashed Opium and Poison. Corporate fat cats and junk bond dealers flung money around as if there were no tomorrow, but there was: Black Monday, October 19, 1987. The stock market crashed and all bets were off. The Gulf War and the spread of AIDS sobered everyone up.

In the early and mid-nineties, in search of safety, comfort, and well-being, the trend turned soft, cocoony, clean, and sheer. The fragrances that fit the profile were Sunflowers, Vanilla Fields, Eternity, Cool Water, and Chloe Innocence. Genders blurred onstage, with entertainers like Ru Paul, or on the court, with basketball star Dennis Rodman. Fragrances were shared; males and females reached for the same bottle of cK One or cK Be.

This was also the era of the delectable or "yummy" scent. Yummy ranged from the teenage-sweet Vanilla Fields by Coty to the more sophisticated scent of Angel by Thierry Mugler, with its innovative chocolate, caramel, and berry accord. The yummy scents capitalized on the comfort factor that food embodies. "People associate food with being taken care of," explains Kathleen Cameron, vice president of creative fragrance development at Takasago, a supplier based in Rockleigh, New Jersey. Think of the mug of hot cocoa your mother brought to you when you were sick and swaddled in blankets. "Fruits and vegetables are the new florals," Cameron asserted as she showed me Takasago's new fruit and vegetable accords. We sat on a sofa in a sparsely decorated office while she dipped blotters one after another. There was the plum tomato accord, young carrot, Italian parsley, sugar beet, and, finally, kadota fig—a sugary sweet scent that reminded me of an afternoon snack. "It's more of a Fig Newton note," Cameron explained. "We were reaching for an interpretation of what people think of a fig rather than its actual smell."

It all seemed so healthy, I commented. After all, I had grown up in an era when "finish your vegetables" was the dictum of the dinner table. Cameron agreed with my observation about the slant toward health and well-being, and pointed out that the vegetable notes were right on target with the trend toward organic foods, nutritive supplements, and herbal medicines. Fashion is fashion, be it platform shoes, naval rings, ginseng capsules, or carrot-scented shampoo. At least there are limits. "For all the health benefits," says Cameron, "a broccoli note just wouldn't work."

And the next big thing?

"Unisex is on the way out," a marketing director for a supplier told me. "The next trend is: 'Don't call it anything. Just make it a fragrance.'

"Transparent is on the way out, too," she continued. "So is depressed and skinny. The economy is good. The stock market is up. Unemployment is down. People are in good spirits. In the ads for Happy and Contradiction they're laughing like mad. Of course we're not happy the way we were in the eighties. We know the bottom can drop out. It's faked happiness: It's perfume Prozac."

On October 28, 1997, Calvin Klein introduced his ninth scent, a woman's fragrance called Contradiction, in Washington, D.C. The event, marked by a cocktail party, was held in the Corcoran Gallery of Art, in an airy atrium bordered by Doric columns made of gray limestone. The invitation on cream-colored stock stated that guests could celebrate the new fragrance as well as "the women of Washington, D.C., who have embraced life's contradictions to achieve the extraordinary."

In keeping with the Calvin Klein image, the cocktail

party was an exercise in monochromatic minimalism. The ambience was spare, ascetic, and sleek. Even the guests, as if in unconscious collusion with the aesthetics of the occasion, dressed in black, white, and beige.

It was a cocktail party envisioned by a Zen Buddhist. Guests were served tiny black, white, and beige bits of food in geometrical shapes. There was sushi in round, oval, and triangle shapes and tiny sphere-like pockets filled with minced duck. The minimalist hors d'oeuvres were passed on black lacquer trays from the Calvin Klein home collection, shipped in from New York for the occasion. The waiters, who were not shipped in, but local, wore black silk Calvin Klein ties on loan for the evening.

As a concession to Washington tastes, which run more to lamb chops and chicken than sushi, there was an hors d'oeuvre of potato-stuffed pastry purses. ("You have to have hearty in Washington," the Klein people were told.)

On a shrine-like table at one end of the room, different ingredients of the perfume were displayed on white china plates, also from the Calvin Klein home collection. At the other end stood a TV screen that displayed a greeting from Calvin Klein himself.

"It's about consistency of image," explained Jan Sharkansky, vice president of global communications for Calvin Klein Cosmetics, as I marveled at the seemingly effortless but intricate choreography of the party.

"We have a protocol," Sharkansky said. "We talk to the caterer beforehand. We talk shapes, size, and arrangement of hors d'oeuvres." A waiter approached us to offer a tray of tiny round rice crackers topped with paper-thin coin, of rare tuna. Sharkansky reached for one and inspected it. "Perfect," she pronounced.

The flowers, several clear glass cylinders with white calla lilies, were quintessential Calvin Klein. "The florist complained it was too simple," Sharkansky reported. "'Look' I said, 'if you think it's too simple, you're on the right track. We're talking minimal.'

"If Calvin Klein were here, he would have taken it to another level. We wouldn't be holding these napkins," she said, indicating the paper napkins we'd been handed with our cocktails. The cocktail glasses—slim, glass flutes—held the only color for miles around: peach-colored, pink-grapefruit-juice-and-champagne cocktails matched to the same shade as Contradiction.

God and Calvin Klein are in the details. Coherence and clarity of image reign supreme. Klein's fashion style is sleek and simple; the hors d'oeuvres should be too. "The general rule for our events is: no sticks, bones, or tails," Sharkansky summed up.

"It's our trunk show," Sheila Hewett, vice president for marketing and advertising, explained to me several months later in her New York office when I expressed admiration for the exquisite attention to detail. "You may not know it, but you've had a complete environmental experience." Everything at the launch, she explained, was designed to reflect the Klein vision and sense of design. Consistency of image; it is one of the trademarks of a successful brand. In Calvin Klein's case, it's the complicated art of utter simplicity.

"We just did events in Hamburg and Paris," Hewett added. "If you were there, you would have seen the same thing." She pulled out a two-inch-thick loose-leaf binder with a silver cover. "This is the book that spells it out," she said, explaining that it set out the script to be followed for the Contradiction launch. The launch parties in New York, Boston, Chicago, Dallas, and Los Angeles—all held within days of each other—would follow the same script as the one in Washington. The silver-covered notebook would ensure the consistency of image.

Meanwhile, the marketing engine would run at full throttle. During the month following the launch parties, more than 20 million scent strips would be nestled between the pages of carefully selected magazines. A million vials with samples of the scent would be handed out in department stores. Advertising featuring model Christy Turlington would be seen on television and in print. In all, according to *Women's Wear Daily*, 9 million dollars would be spent on promotion in hopes of shipping out 30 to 40 million dollars' worth of the new fragrance in its first year.

Will Contradiction still be around in, say, ten years? Will it make a bundle, only to fade into the fragrance sunset after a couple of years? Will it do the unthinkable: lose money?

Let the dice roll.

"All the world's a mall," says an industry consultant, who would not be quoted for attribution. "Fifth Avenue is a mall. The Champs-Élysées is a mall. They want to sell as much of the same thing to as many people as possible. There's this great homogenizing force. It can get pretty boring."

The buzzword is global: There's a scurry to new markets prompted by a saturated domestic market. From 1996 to 1997, according to Euromonitor, an international market analyst, the industry registered about a two percent increase in United States sales, barely a bump. "The problem is one of minimal growth," says Marlene Eskin, a marketing consultant based in Austin, Texas, who follows the industry. For the past ten years revenues in the industry are for the most part flat. In this country, and much of Europe, the market, as they say, has matured.

The frontier of growth lies farther abroad; Eastern Europe, China, and South America are big. Saudi Arabia has perhaps the highest per capita use, more than a quart a year. (In Saudi Arabia, an Islamic country where alcohol is forbidden, the tops of perfume bottles must be permanently affixed—presumably to prevent a perfume from being turned into a cocktail.) Japan is a longed-for market, but a headache for many. "The Japanese give a status symbol perfume as a gift. Then it sits on the shelf," frets Dominique Goby of Systems Bio-Industrie, an essential oil producer.

On the other hand, Spain is a fragrance company's dream. "In Spain soap is perfumed at a three-percent concentration," Goby enthused. "In the rest of Europe it's five percent. The Spanish perfume their babies, and cologne comes in liter-size bottles."

According to a report on global tastes, done by Esther Morera for the Fragrance Foundation, a New York–based organization that promotes the use of fragrance, Korean women prefer florals. The Spanish prefer citrus. The French like full, rich fragrances and animal notes. Americans go for sweet, fruity, florals. And the Japanese remain a puzzle. The Japanese don't use a lot of perfume. To stand out of the crowd by smelling of something loud and strong, however beautiful, is not a virtue in that culture, though a younger, hipper, generation may change all that.

The era of the family-run company has faded. Only Chanel, owned by the Wertheimer family of Paris, and Jean Patou, owned by the de Moüy family, also Paris-based, are left. Nearly everyone else has been absorbed by a multinational giant or, like the Lauders, taken the family business and turned it into a publicly owned corporation. Who owns what? In the era of multinational companies, working out the lineage of a fragrance company can be a challenge.

Unilever, the Anglo-Dutch consumer products giant, owns Calvin Klein Cosmetics and Elizabeth Arden. The Estée Lauder Companies, a virtual fiefdom of fragrance, includes the Estée Lauder line of scents, as well as fragrances produced by its Clinique, Aramis, Prescriptives, Bobbi Brown, and Origins divisions, not to mention licensing agreements with Donna Karan and Tommy Hilfiger. A license, a common industry arrangement, grants exclusive rights to a company to use a name or likeness in producing a fragrance. Examples of fragrance licenses include Lauder's agreement with Tommy Hilfiger and Bijan's agreement with Michael Jordan. Creative approval, quality, pricing, marketing, advertising, and distribution are all governed by the contract and differ on a case-by-case basis. The licensor, like Lauder, takes the risk; the licensee like Hilfiger, provides the star power.

Elf Aquitaine, the French petrochemical giant, owns most of the cosmetics company Sanofi Beauté, which has Yves Saint Laurent and Oscar de la Renta fragrances under

Objects of art and high bidding, antique perfume bottles await auction by Phillips Auctioneers of Geneva, Switzerland. This collection ranges from whimsical glassworks in the form of elephants, dogs, and torsos, to sophisticated clean lines and fancy stoppers. One of the leaders in 20th century flacon design was René Lalique, who brought unusual colors and shapes to the art of the bottle.

its wing. The French luxury goods conglomerate LVMH owns—among other jewels—Dior, Givenchy, and Guerlain. The Japanese cosmetics giant Shiseido owns Paris-based Beauté Prestige International, which has produced two big hits: L'Eau d'Issey and Jean-Paul Gaultier.

And, in a particularly intricate bit of fragrance/business genealogy, the Swiss food products company Nestlé has a slice of the French company L'Oréal. And L'Oréal, in turn, through its United States subsidiary, Cosmair, owns European Designer Fragrances, which markets Acqua di Giò, Drakkar Noir, Paloma Picasso, Anaïs Anaïs, and Arpège.

"Isn't that confusing, not to mention, incestuous?" I asked Fernando Aleu, chairman of Compar, which sells fragrance for Carolina Herrara, as well as Paco Rabanne. After all, wasn't a company competing with itself if it had dozens of fragrances in its repertory?

The question elicited a smile. "You have to pretend to be virtuous while being promiscuous," he replied.

In this global arena, the two big players—and rivals—are France and the United States.

Where is the center of the fragrance universe?

"Paris," says Patrick Choël, president of Christian Dior Parfums. A gaunt, pale man, he sits in a lipstick-red leather Le Corbusier chair in his Paris office. "Americans are safe, not experimental," he says, softly and very, very fast. "When you look at some of the successful American brands, you get a lot of crap. There is nothing more conventional than the United States student. They wear Nikes, jeans, and drink Coke. Cheap, simple, basic. That's the reason for Calvin Klein's success. He sells the American lifestyle. We are Dior. We cannot be like that. We are selling the ultimate French good taste."

Dominick Anastasio, president of Fashion Fragrances & Cosmetics, downs a swallow of coffee in the Edwardian Room of New York's Plaza Hotel and counters in flat, raspy New Yorkese. "The French lost their derrieres after World War II. They refused to accept that 'Made in France' means almost nothing except to a few women anymore." He singles out American entrepreneurs like Estée Lauder and Charles Revson, founder of Revlon, who helped shift the center of gravity from France to the United States with affordable, accessible scents like Youth Dew and Charlie.

Revlon's Charlie was a sensation when introduced in 1973. Wearable day or night, it spoke to the lifestyle of the liberated woman. When Charles Revson, who didn't allow pants in his offices, showed a woman striding in pants in the ads, he tapped right into the social shift of the decade. In the years to follow the lifestyle fragrance became an American specialty, culminating in scents that expressed a mood, a trend, a cultural zeitgeist, like Calvin Klein's Eternity, cK One, and cK Be. The language of lifestyle is contemporary, and it sells. "The French don't understand this market," says Dominick Anastasio. "They have lost."

At a 1995 industry conference in Grasse, the tug-of-war erupted in public. The Americans went first and spoke of positioning and how well they understood the global market. Then the French took their turn and just as stridently claimed they were the center of creativity and experimentation.

After much puffing from both sides, Serge Lutens, a designer of cosmetics and creator of perfumes who has an exquisite perfumerie in Paris, spoke of mysteries and secrets: the soul of perfume. He spoke of how, in Morocco, you can get drunk on smelling roses. He spoke of Marie Antoinette in her carriage—the people knew it was her by the scent of her carriage passing in the street. He spoke of Cleopatra and myrrh, and how you can tell the whole of human history through perfume. Afterward, a perfumer in the audience stood up and said, "At last, someone speaks of perfume."

So let us speak of perfume and a magic that beguiles us into believing our dreams will come true. Let us remember that the only thing that matters is the beauty in the bottle and a fragrance that moves us to tears.

The design and creation of perfume flacons is an industry in itself. Large perfume companies spend small fortunes on their bottles, which act as three-dimensional interpretations of the promise within.

From Coco Chanel
to
Michael Jordan

"So what if Chanel No. 5 were launched today?" I ask Ann Gottlieb, the New York consultant, one day at lunch. "How would it do?"

"Oh, it probably wouldn't be a smashing success," she says thoughtfully. "It's difficult to get into. It's got an old-fashioned top note—floral aldehyde. But once you're into it, it's glorious in wear, and I think the market is forgiving of it because of what it is."

"Which is?" I prompt.

"A piece of history."

A piece of *elusive* history. There is myth, there is reality, and there is an in-between realm where boundaries blur.

"She made up things," Axel Madsen, one of Coco Chanel's biographers, said. She continually revised her life story. She transformed a vagrant, absent father into a respectable horse trader. She denied she had brothers and sisters. She fogged even the most rudimentary facts of her life with fabrications.

"Could I ask you where you were born?" asked Edmonde Charles-Roux, another biographer. Chanel named a town that never existed.

She was the illegitimate daughter of a peddler, born on August 19, 1883, in Saumur, a town on the Loire in the heart of France. Her mother died when she was 12, and her father abandoned her. She was raised in an orphanage in the provinces. It was a period of her life she never discussed. Born without a background, she felt compelled to invent one. She gave herself the patina of an imagined history.

"She was a peasant and a genius," said Diana Vreeland, the doyenne of fashion editors, who was not above autobiographical embroidery herself. "Peasants and geniuses are the only people who count, and she was both."

She was a peasant by birth and character. She loved working with her hands. "If I were not embarrassed to be seen, I would love to shoe a horse," she once told a friend. She would take fabric in hand, reach for pins in a bowl held by an assistant, and, scissors flashing, shape it into one of her signature suits right on the model. Never mind the models wilting with fatigue, she wouldn't stop until the sleeves were perfectly set, the silhouette sufficiently trim, the hemline set just below the knee. She could explode with impatience: She could toss an improperly sewn bow right back in a seamstress's face; her tongue could scald. "I adore you," she reportedly said to designer Christian Dior, "but you dress

To celebrate its 75th anniversary, Chanel packaged No. 5 in a special edition box decorated with an Andy Warhol silk-screen print. The strategy reaffirmed its status as an icon while updating its image.

women like armchairs." When she died in 1971 at the age of 87, she was working on her spring collection.

She was a genius. She dressed women in modern, comfortable clothes. She put women in pants and told them they could wear black every day. She dressed them in easy-to-wear knit suits, bell-bottom trousers, and pea jackets. She gave us the quilted bag and the two-tone sling-back pump. She used fabrics, notably jersey and tweed, that no one but men wore. "I don't create fashion; I create style," she said.

Finally, she introduced Chanel No. 5—perhaps the most familiar perfume in the world—an icon and true classic. In a world where the fragrance du jour changes with the rapidity of hemlines, Chanel No. 5 murmurs of good taste in the same way that the dark, rich gleam of heirloom silver bespeaks good breeding.

Was the idea of doing a perfume that of her closest friend, Misia Sert? Did the inspiration, as others suggest, come at the suggestion of her young lover, the Russian Grand Duke Dmitri Pavlovich Romanov? Or perhaps she woke up one morning and decided to create a perfume. Think what you will. Anyway, in 1920, Coco Chanel and a perfumer named Ernest Beaux met in his laboratory in Grasse and collaborated on a perfume that would be a bestseller three-quarters of a century later.

"I want something that reflects my personality, something abstract and unique, a perfume of regal discretion, to form a halo of light around my clothes," Chanel reportedly said. She was fearless, unafraid to be different. "I want a perfume that is composed. It's a paradox. On a woman a natural flower scent smells artificial. Perhaps a natural perfume must be created artificially," she told Beaux.

Beaux gave her ten (some say seven, some eight—again, the scrim screen of myth obscures our view) fragrances to choose from. She chose number five. She named her fragrance Chanel No. 5. Chanel No. 5: The name was simple and straightforward like Chanel herself.

Use the best ingredients, Chanel told Ernest Beaux. And he did, pouring in lavish, costly amounts of *absolue jasmin de Grasse, rose de mai,* sandalwood, iris, and ylang-ylang. The composition was rich beyond belief, and then, says Jacques Polge, the chief perfumer for Chanel, Beaux had the idea of using a great big splash of aldehydes, an overdose of one percent in fact, to give these glorious natural floral oils lift, and to make the fragrance modern, contemporary, and clean—just like the couture that made her famous. "It's like doing a detailed drawing," Polge explains. "Then smudging it to make it more abstract, less literal."

Like everything else about Coco Chanel and Chanel No. 5, the overdose of aldehyde—a powerful synthetic with an astringent scent—has its own litany of myths. A popular story says the overdose was the mistake of a laboratory assistant, who added ten times the amount actually called for. Others say Beaux knew exactly what he was doing. And Beaux himself? Years later, when asked about his use of aldehydes in Chanel No. 5, he reportedly slid past the question with an enigmatic remark about how it was best to use new materials in equal proportions.

However it happened, it was a bold stroke and it was brilliant. "No one has gone beyond No. 5," Diana Vreeland once said, with Vreelandesque finality. But, of course, many people have—after all, tastes change. But for its time—the 1920s—no one had gone beyond Chanel 5. Before Chanel No. 5 aldehydes were a novelty. No perfume had ever used them in any significant way. Chanel No. 5 was a first. "Aldehydes give a solid, luminous foundation, a canvas as solid as the side of a house, on to which you can paint abstract olfactory forms," explains Luca Turin, a London-based biophysicist and author of *Parfum: Le Guide.*

The scent was launched in 1921, without advertising, Marie-Louise de Clermont-Tonnerre, general director of public relations for Chanel in Paris, tells me. "Chanel No. 5 was born in Grasse, but it was sold for the first time in Paris."

*Dripping with her trademark ropes of pearls, Coco Chanel poses with characteristic bravura
on a couch. Chanel mixed real jewels with fake; the trend in costume jewelry is one of her legacies.
"Nothing looks more fake than a real jewel," she liked to say.*

It was introduced casually, with great cunning, according to Pierre Galante, another biographer. Coco Chanel gave away hundreds of bottles to her best clients, then, when asked where they could get more, would feign wide-eyed surprise. "The perfume? What perfume? Oh, yes, the little bottle I gave you yesterday. You want to buy some? My dear, I don't sell perfume. I found the bottles almost by chance in Grasse. . . ."

Or, equally as disingenuously: "You think I should have some made and sell it? You like my perfume that much?"

She made certain its scent permeated every corner of the boutique, from the front door to the fitting rooms. "The doorman at the Ritz where she slept would phone, and I know this for myself because I was told by someone who was there," de Clermont-Tonnerre said. The word would go out: *Mademoiselle arrive!* A salesgirl would immediately dash around the boutique and up the spiral staircase frantically spraying an atomizer of Chanel No. 5 around the premises, trailing clouds of perfume in her wake.

In 1924 Coco Chanel and Pierre Wertheimer, owner of Bourjois, the largest cosmetics and fragrance company at the time in France, formed Parfums Chanel in a deal that gave Coco ownership of her couture business as a separate company and ten percent of the profits from the perfume. Although she always lived stylishly and well, the decision would gall her the rest of her life. Forever after clouds of resentment, contention, and legal suits marked the relationship between the designer and the businessman.

"Without quite realizing the long-term implications of what she was doing, Coco Chanel had signed away the most profitable potential of her business for a relative pittance," Phyllis Berman wrote in *Forbes* magazine. Today, the Wertheimer family owns and controls all of the business, including all rights to the Chanel name.

The original Chanel boutique stands at 31 Rue Cambon, one of those sun-deprived, narrow streets of wall-to-wall chic on the Right Bank of Paris. The windows of the store frame a medley of interlocking C's, the ubiquitous Chanel insignia, which appears on everything from beach towels to sandals to the buttons of the exquisite wool suits that made Chanel so famous. Inside, Japanese teenagers in blue jeans and French matrons in their tan and black Chanel pumps linger at the perfume counter to sample a fragrance or leaf through racks of beautifully cut suits in the ready-to-wear department.

Chanel's apartment is hidden away on the third floor, and I am sitting with Véronique de Pardieu, its curator, on the fawn-colored velvet couch in the living room. There is a fine-tuned empathy between the elegantly French de Pardieu, who has the impeccable diction of British nanny-taught English, and the woman whose apartment she watches over. "I feel protective of her," de Pardieu says of Chanel. "She's here." It seems as if it must be so. There is an ormolu-mounted writing desk at the side of the room and on it rest Chanel's sunglasses, as if she had just set them down the minute before.

If Chanel really were here, the room would have

ABOVE *Coco Chanel surveys her mannequins—the models who provided the forms on which she created and displayed her clothes. Fittings could last six to eight hours, and through it all Chanel remained indefatiguable.*
OPPOSITE *Difficult, demanding, obsessively perfectionist, Chanel adjusts a dress in her 1966 collection.*

flowers—white camellias and gardenias with their rich, heady scent. "She liked big pieces in small rooms," de Pardieu says, indicating the massively ornate Venetian mirrors gracing the fireplace mantle and the antique Chinese coromandel screens that decorate the rooms. The apartment has no bedroom; Chanel slept at the Ritz, its back door across the street from her boutique. But she lived her daily life and entertained guests here, on the third floor, amidst the exquisite coromandel screens. "She couldn't bear to be alone," de Pardieu says. "She would hide the door by placing a screen in front of it, so her guests couldn't leave."

She loved beautiful things and her friends fed this passion. The composer Igor Stravinsky gave her a Russian icon. Other friends—Salvador Dalí, Alberto Giacometti—gave other mementos. She loved lions—she was a Leo, born in August—so lions in bronze, crystal, and jade lie scattered all over the room. In the corner of the foyer is a life-sized, 18th-century bronze Chinese statue of a deer. "She loved animals," de Pardieu, says. "Chanel said they always cured her pain."

And there was plenty of pain for Coco Chanel, especially when it came to love. Arthur "Boy" Capel, a rich polo-playing Englishman, described by friends as the great love of her life, died in an automobile accident. Paul Iribe, a painter she was reportedly engaged to in the thirties, died of a heart attack while playing tennis at her villa on the Riviera. "She was living, hoping the right man would ask her the right question—will you marry me?" said biographer Edmonde Charles-Roux. It never happened. Near the end of her life, she was bitter. "I never knew what happiness was," she told an interviewer in 1966. "When I was a child, I sought love; I didn't get it. Later, undoubtedly, I found more love than I wanted."

But not, perhaps, the kind she sought. She found fame instead. But even being the fashion spirit of the 20th century had its limits. She hid away from her own shows. "It wasn't shyness; she couldn't be bothered," de Pardieu

believes. When her clothes were being shown in the salon, she would sit at the top of the art deco staircase that curls back on itself four times. From her perch she could see the salon below, reflected in the staircase mirror. As I write this I am looking at a photograph, by the Japanese photographer Hatami, of Chanel sitting in that very spot. She is wearing her trademark pearls, hat, and oversized glasses. She sits in shadowed profile, gazing in the mirror at the whirl of fashion she has created. She looks reflective and removed, almost distant from the world of elegance unfurling in the salon below.

The searing remark, the temper, the studied diffidence of the woman hiding on the staircase during her shows, mask vulnerability in the same way she used her coromandel screens to hide the door. She was clever, complex, and, says de Pardieu, "so very, very vulnerable."

Behind locked doors, in a climate-controlled room deep in a basement in Neuilly, a fashionable suburb of Paris, in a nondescript building that is the headquarters of Parfums Chanel, a highly animated mop-haired man in a brown-checked suit and silk tie pulls on a pair of white gloves. And, like a magician about to pull a rabbit out of a hat, he offers a small, white box for my inspection.

"I present to you the first No. 5," Pierre Buntz, curator of the perfume archives, says, with a sly smile.

"It's a bit off-white, like cooked eggs." He is commenting on the small box he is carefully opening; the bleached white of the present-day box would come much later on. Buntz slips out a match box-sized bottle with a label no bigger than my thumbnail. It reads "CHANEL" in capital block letters centered on the label, with "No. 5" in small letters above, and "Paris" in small letters below.

The glass bottle is not yet faceted, that would come three years later, in 1924, but the basic shape—the bones—are there. The bottle, like the box, is absolutely plain, unornamented, except for the black and white of the

Evolution of a classic: The design of the Chanel No. 5 bottle has been subtly modified five times in the past seven decades. The update allows the bottle to remain contemporary in look, in concordance with the design sensibility of the era.

print. It is the little black dress of perfume bottles. It is also, Jacques Polge, chief perfumer for Chanel, points out, the Rolls Royce of bottles. The materials are basic: cardboard, unornamented glass, and paper. The package and its bottle is a haiku in black and white—black letters, white label, white box. "How much more difficult to be simple," Buntz muses.

"Her idea was that the bottle should be a container and protect the perfume," Jacques Helleu tells me later that day in his office. Helleu, a tall, imposing man with a great sweep of silver hair, is design director of Parfums Chanel, as was his father before him. He is the guardian, the steward, of Chanel No. 5's image and look.

The idea for the bottle came from a man's toilette kit, Helleu explains. The bottle is simple and totally functional. Stripped of the superfluous, it does what it is supposed to and no more. It contains perfume.

And it always looks contemporary. Why? Every twenty years or so the bottle is ever so slightly modified to update and ease it into its new era. It's a small change, often so subtle the customer doesn't even notice. "The idea," Helleu says, "is to parallel what is happening in the outside world. At the end of the 1940s, when refrigerators were very large and the bumpers of cars like Studebaker had round noses, the bottle itself got bigger and rounder. In the seventies we go a bit flatter, with more angles, and the stopper becomes slightly bigger. It comes on the heels of the era of the clean lines of architects like Eero Saarinen.

"Chanel didn't know she would create a tremendous success. She just wanted to be simple," he points out.

But 75 years—that's a long time to be such a big seller. Chanel No. 5 always sits somewhere in the top five selling fragrances in the world. Thousands of perfumes have come and gone, and some of them have been very, very good. So why has Chanel No. 5 survived?

"Advertising," Helleu promptly replies. "That's the key. Creativity in advertising. To be audacious. Chanel is the first company to do TV in the fragrance industry, and one of the first to use a personality like Catherine Deneuve or Carole Bouquet to promote itself."

Chanel No. 5 is constantly being reinvented in astonishing ways. In 1996, to celebrate its 75th anniversary, the company packaged the perfume in a box decorated with Andy Warhol's silk-screen print of a bottle of No. 5. It was fresh, fun, and totally irresistible.

"Please, isn't it too much?" said the director of marketing for a competitor in near-reverential admiration. "It's interesting how you can revitalize a long-standing brand like that. Try doing that in two years with Cool Water Woman."

And who could forget Marilyn Monroe's famous line.

"What do you sleep in Miss Monroe?" an interviewer asked.

"Chanel No. 5," she replied.

"A gift," Jacques Helleu calls her response. How could you ever buy such publicity?

It was one icon endorsing another.

More than 75 years have passed since the introduction of Chanel No. 5. The world has changed; tastes change. Fragrance is market-driven. No, not even that, says an industry executive: "It's marketing-driven." If something is market-driven, you're giving people what they want; marketing-driven means creating a desire not there to begin with. You can almost put on a Broadway show for less than you can launch a scent. Fragrances, with a few exceptions, are created by perfumers, who work for suppliers. The French jasmine and French *rose de mai* in Chanel No. 5 are out-of-reach expensive to all but a very few perfumes.

Perfumers are asked to create a winning scent in weeks, and submissions are subject to interminable market testing. As part of marketing strategy and "positioning," perfumes have a story line—even those that did not start their lives with one. Take Shalimar, a celebration of "the eternal love"

of an Indian emperor, or Mitsouko, "an impossible love story" about a beautiful Japanese girl married to an admiral but secretly loved by a British officer. In the beginning "we had no story about Shalimar or Mitsouko," says Jean-Paul Guerlain, grandson of Jacques Guerlain, creator of both. "But we did the same thing as the others."

On October 27, 1996, I visit Macy's on 34th Street in New York, where a new cologne is to debut. Sally Yeh, president of Bijan Fragrances, the company that has licensed and is marketing the scent, patrols the aisles of the cosmetics department, inspecting the layout, watching preparations like a hawk. The product about to be unveiled epitomizes the fragrance-as-aspirational approach. It's Michael Jordan cologne, the latest contender in the celebrity fragrance sweepstakes.

"We're hoping it will be the Young Spice," Yeh says, alluding to Old Spice, one of the best-selling mass-market men's fragrances of all time. Jordan, the megastar basketball player for the Chicago Bulls, has licenses galore for sports equipment and clothing, but the foray into fragrance is new ground.

Yeh notes the red carpet in the aisles and makes sure it is straight. She asks that a huge vase of red calla lilies sitting on a counter be moved—they obscure the Michael Jordan poster. She checks out the counters full of boxes of the new cologne. She nods approvingly at the huge black-and-red cutout with Jordan's unmistakable silhouette. She greets the head buyer of the department and pulls him off to the side for a private chat.

By this time of year the Christmas decorations should be up in the store, Yeh tells me, but she has prevailed on the management to wait so as not to interfere with the Jordan launch.

She put Santa Claus on hold?

"I have a healthy disregard for the impossible," she responds with a low chuckle.

Advertising spending for the first year is around 22 million dollars. There will be TV and print ads, billboards,

The secret spectator, Coco Chanel watches her clothes parade by at one of her shows in the Rue Cambon boutique.
From her perch on the spiral staircase she could see but remain unseen. Illegitimately born, raised as an orphan,
the role of outsider came naturally to her. "I don't create fashion," she said. "I create style." Among her innovations
are classics like the two-toned pump, the jersey suit, and the little black dress.

and radio spots, and it doesn't hurt that Michael Jordan's movie, *Space Jam*, is about to open. In fact, Yeh moved the launch forward by a month to catch that wave.

Unlike Chanel No. 5, which started its commercial life in one place only, the boutique at 31 Rue Cambon, Michael Jordan will debut in 3,500 stores, or "doors," as the industry calls them, including Foot Locker, a pioneer marketing move based on the theory that anyone who walks into an athletic shoe store is primed to buy anything with the Jordan name on it.

The Jordan fragrance will target the new, big-disposable-income segment of the market, Generation-Xers from 20 to 31 and their up-and-coming successors, teenagers from 12 to 19. The operative word is cool. "The Michael Jordan fragrance," the positioning statement reads, "will provide our audience with an opportunity to 'enjoy a part of Michael.' The fragrance is hip and upscale, yet not over-the-top and out-of-reach." The bottle for the Jordan cologne, clear glass, curvilinear-shaped, impressed with a basketball and sneaker-tread bottom, was designed even before the "juice" was a gleam in the perfumer's eye. The price of a bottle is $23, the number Jordan wears on his jersey.

Instead of the ten or so submissions Ernest Beaux gave Coco Chanel to choose from, Sally Yeh and her staff briefed five suppliers and looked at more than 600 submissions from 25 perfumers. "And that's a conservative number," she says. But that's just the tip of the submission iceberg. Each of the five suppliers in the race evaluated hundreds and hundreds of scents by their perfumers before selecting their best-shot contenders for the Jordan brief.

In contrast to Coco Chanel and Ernest Beaux, Michael Jordan's contact with the perfumers who worked on the fragrance bearing his name was negligible. "We never talked to him (Jordan) directly, but the Bijan people had a good handle on his lifestyle and personality," Steve De Mercado,

the Givaudan Roure perfumer who created the winning fragrance, told me. The cologne he created for Jordan is cool and crisp, with citrus top notes, lavender, juniper, and fir for freshness, and an undertone of musk and woods.

The Jordan brief, dubbed "project double-dribble," by Givaudan Roure, involved six of their perfumers; two account executives; six compounders; one person in stability testing; two sensory psychologists; two people in consumer research; three scientists in applied research, and at least six staffers in other roles like marketing and project management. It was fast track all the way. Six months after handing out the brief, Sally Yeh called Geoffrey Webster, Givaudan Roure's president of fragrance worldwide, to say that his group had won. The victory was celebrated with champagne at Givaudan Roure's United States headquarters in Teaneck, New Jersey.

"Domestic or imported?" I asked Webster.

"We're a French company," he replied. "We drink French champagne—vintage Veuve Cliquot."

Although Jordan never spoke to the perfumers who worked on his cologne, he had a hand in the final selection, Yeh says. The person from the Jordan camp with the most presence in the project was probably his agent, David Falk, who represents a block of the top players in pro basketball. With stars like Michael Jordan and Patrick Ewing under his fiduciary wing, Falk, reported the *New York Times*, is considered the second most powerful person in the National Basketball Association after its commissioner.

"A Michael Jordan fragrance?" I asked Falk as we sat in his Washington office. I'd seen tapes of Jordan's promotional talk show blitz tour (he doesn't do store appearances, he'd cause a riot, Falk says), and Jay Leno and David Letterman predictably went to town on the idea of a Michael Jordan fragrance that stank of sweaty socks.

"It's because Michael is named to the best dressed list, he's concerned with and fond of his appearance," Falk

Selling the brand is the name of the fragrance game. In this case, the brand is Michael Jordan, a figure so recognizable that a silhouette of his head is all the potential customer needs to identify him.

explains. "I thought it would be a natural extension of someone who is an arbiter of style. It wasn't like we were looking to make more deals."

"What is the deal?" I ask.

"Michael will do whatever it takes reasonably to make the fragrance a success," he replies. "And he'll get a percentage of the sales."

"How much of a percentage?"

"I've made deals from half of one percent to 50 percent," Falk says.

"Where does this particular deal fall on that spectrum?"

"Somewhere in between," he replies. "Michael Jordan is the best-known, most popular figure on earth by any marketing standard. In China he's more recognized than Chou En-lai. My guess is that they [Bijan Fragrances] will cover the entire guarantee in the first year."

"Guarantee?"

"We have as a screening method, a base minimum." He means that even to get in the licensing game with Jordan there's big-time up-front money to be paid.

"Which is?"

"Very substantial."

"Hundreds of thousands?" I guess.

"Millions."

As my 12-year-old son might say, we're talking awesome numbers. "Michael transcended sports years ago," Falk says, adding that even when Jordan retires from the basketball court, it won't mean a thing. "If anything, he'll be bigger." Jordan, I finally understand, is not just an athlete. He's a brand, so instantly recognizable that the logo on the box of Michael Jordan cologne is a small red-and-black silhouette of his head. That's all that is needed for instant recognition—his silhouette. "It's the age of The Brand,"

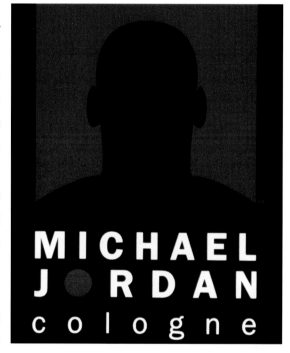

Sharon Osen, a branding strategy consultant based in New York, tells me. "At our agency we have a saying: God is Dead. Brands are God." Michael Jordan, the brand, is total dream.

It's obviously hopeless, but I make one last stab at finding out the percentage Jordan will earn from the sale of the cologne.

"The percentage figures?" I ask.

Falk glances at his watch. "A lot. He's making a lot."

But will Michael Jordan cologne have, as they say in show business, legs as long as its namesake? According to NPD Beauty *Trends*, a marketing research firm that tracks department store sales of fine fragrance, domestic sales of the Jordan cologne have dropped in the year following its highly successful 1996 launch. For the month of December 1996, two months after its launch, department store sales were about nine million dollars. A year later, sales for the month of December 1997, totaled about five million dollars. These totals do not reflect the additional revenue generated by sales at Foot Locker and venues other than specialty and department stores, but the drop is typical of the dip fragrances take after the luster of a launch has dimmed.

"Typically, you see a brand's highest sales when it comes out," says Timra Carlson of NPD. "Consumer interest is at its height. The goal is to maintain sales at a high level for a long time." The answer lies in supporting the brand with continued advertising, also expanding into international markets. Ultimately it's about finding ways to deal with the short attention span of the customer. "It's always about entertainment," Sally Yeh says.

"We kind of fell in love with ourselves and decided we didn't need to be as promotional," Yeh admits, when I asked about the dip in sales. The lapse was quickly corrected, she says. Whereas in its first year much of the Jordan advertising was broadcast media, now the cologne will be seriously advertised in print. Another venue will be "bus wraps" on New York City buses. Already, the cologne has been introduced in Europe, the Middle East, and Asia. Line extensions like soap and body gel have been introduced. Distribution has been broadened into stores like J. C. Penney and mail-order catalogs. Even so, there is no sure thing. "One success does not guarantee the next," she says. In the fragrance business, as in basketball, you win some; you lose some.

Not surprisingly, Yeh remains optimistic. "Will Michael Jordan cologne still be around in 75 years?" I ask her.

"Of course," she replies. "By then it will be an all-time classic, just like the man himself. And, for that matter, Chanel No. 5 will be 150 years old."

Three-quarters of a century later, in the era of The Brand, Chanel No. 5 and Michael Jordan turn out, in some ways, to be not too dissimilar after all. The fragrance industry mantra, Support the Brand, applies to both. Whether it's the flash of Warhol packaging for Chanel No. 5's 75th anniversary, or a pitch for Michael Jordan cologne on the side of a New York City bus, the business is not just about getting—it's about keeping—your product in the eye, and under the nose, of the customer.

Yet, of course, the two fragrances are not the same. The difference between Chanel No. 5 and Michael Jordan cologne is the difference between haute cuisine and a trip to McDonald's, I tell Sally Yeh on the phone. I explain that I'm comparing the history of the two scents to show the difference 75 years has made in the fragrance industry. Big Macs are easy, a quick fix for the stomach and affordable. A five-course meal on linen and fine china might be more pleasing to the palate and eye, but it's costly and not an everyday kind of thing. It's not that one is necessarily better than the other, I tell her. It's just that they're, well, different. It's a matter of style.

Yeh sums it up in two sentences: "Chanel No. 5 developed from romantic imagination; Michael Jordan cologne was based on lifestyle interpretation."

On the ground floor of Macy's department store on 34th Street in Manhattan, seven fragrance models hired for the launch are armed with cologne and poised for action. "Try Michael Jordan cologne. Michael in a bottle," they coo. Some shoppers brush them off impatiently; some eagerly offer their wrists. A ten-year-old in baggy jeans and Adidas goes by and pumps his arm—"Yes!"—at the invitation to try the scent. A young man in his teens wearing a Chicago Bulls T-shirt lingers by the counter passing a blotter strip of the fragrance back and forth under his nose. He seems lost in thought, lost in dreams perhaps of the ultimate slam-dunk basket.

As the day progresses a woman stops when approached by one of the models, a tall, handsome young man with a majestic tangle of braids.

"Only 23 dollars," he teases.

"I don't have a man to give it to," sighs Denise Gordon, a Manhattan teacher.

"Don't wait for a man," he urges.

She coolly looks him up and down, then says, "Put some on, baby, and let me check it out."

He obliges, and before you can say "personal foul," she grabs him and they whirl down the aisle, her face lit up like a Broadway marquee. For a Cinderella instant, the store is transformed into a ballroom.

Does the world really need a new fragrance?

Perhaps. Held up against the sad weight of the world, perfume can seem ultimately frivolous. A whiff of costly air. The essence of illusion.

Viewed against that same sad weight, perfume can be wondrously evocative. An elixir to make us forget. Or remember. Or dream.

Michael Jordan, superstar basketball player for the Chicago Bulls, has plenty of license and endorsement deals with sports-related companies, but the fragrance business is a new arena for him. Michael Jordan, here with his namesake scent in midair, teamed up with Bijan Fragrances to introduce a cologne in the fall of 1996.

B I B L I O G R A P H Y

Ackerman, Diane. *A Natural History of the Senses*. New York: Vintage Books, 1990.

Aleu, Fernando. "Remembering Diana Vreeland." *Beauty Fashion*, April 1997, 95.

Allure, May 1993, 163–165, "Big Night Out."

Barille, Elizabeth, and Catherine Laroze. *The Book of Perfume*. Paris: Flammarion, 1995.

Beauty Facts 1996/1997 Directory. New York: The Ledes Group, Inc., 1986.

Beauty Fashion, September 1996, 142, "Yvresse At Yves Saint Laurent."

Berman, Phyllis, and Zina Sawaya. "The Billionaires Behind Chanel." *Forbes*, April 3,1989, 104–108.

Born, Pete. "Calvin's Contradictory Impulse." *Women's Wear Daily*, June 27,1997, 4.

Born, Pete. "When Launch Fever Becomes the Norm." *Women's Wear Daily*, January 24,1997, 10.

Campbell, Roy H. "Out of it: 'Heroin Chic' Draws Fire From Anti-Drug Groups." *St. Louis Post-Dispatch*, November 28,1996, 13.

Charles-Roux, Edmonde. *Chanel: Her Life, Her World—and the Woman Behind the Legend She Created*. Translated by Nancy Amphoux. NY: Alfred A. Knopf, 1975.

Chilton, Meredith. "A Fugitive Pleasure: Perfume in the 18th Century." *Rotunda*, Summer 1989, 41–45.

Corbin, Alain. *The Foul and the Fragrant: Odor and the French Social Imagination*. Cambridge, MA: Harvard University Press, 1986.

Dayagi-Mendels, Michel. *Perfumes and Cosmetics In the Ancient World*. Tel Aviv: Sabinsky Press Ltd., 1989.

The Economist, July 2,1994, 78, "The Secret Life of Flowers."

The Economist, August 30,1997, 59–61, "Birds do it, Bees do it . . ."

Edwards, Michael. *Perfume Legends: French Feminine Fragrances*. Italy: HM Editions, 1996.

Enrico, Dottie. "Calvin Klein Fragrance Ads Create A Big Stink." *USA Today*, January 6,1997, 14B.

Euromonitor. *The World Market for Fragrances*. London: Euromonitor, February 1997.

The Fragrance Foundation and the Olfactory Research Fund. *The Fragrance & Olfactory Dictionary*. New York: The Fragrance Foundation and the Olfactory Research Fund, Ltd., 1994.

The Fragrance Foundation. *The Fragrance Foundation Reference Guide*. New York: The Fragrance Foundation, 1996.

"The Fragrant Past: Perfumes of Cleopatra and Julius Caesar." Exhibition at Emory University Museum of Art and Archaeology, Michael C. Carlos Hall, Atlanta, Georgia, April 5–June 25, 1989.

Galante, Pierre. *Mademoiselle Chanel*. Translated by Eileen Geist and Jessie Wood. Chicago: Henry Regnery Company, 1973.

Gaudoin, Tina. "Gio Public." *Harper's Bazaar*, February 1993, 36.

Gibbons, Boyd. "The Intimate Sense of Smell." NATIONAL GEOGRAPHIC, September 1986, 324–361.

Graham, Paul G., and Sarah P. Adam. *Les Flacons de la Séduction*. Paris: La Bibliothèque des Arts, 1986.

Green, Timothy. "Making Scents Is More Complicated Than You'd Think." *Smithsonian*, June 1991, 52–60.

Groom, Nigel. *The Perfume Handbook*. London: Chapman and Hall, 1992.

Hirschberg, Lynn. "The Big Man Can Deal." *The New York Times Magazine*, November 17, 1996, 46–88.

Hyde, Nina. "The World of Coco Chanel: Charles Roux Unravels the Cinderella Legend." *The Washington Post*, November 27, 1981, D:1, 14–15.

Hwang, Suein L. "Marketing: Seeking Scents That No One Has Smelled." *Wall Street Journal*, August 10, 1994, 1 (B).

Israel, Lee. *Estée Lauder: Beyond the Magic*. New York: Macmillan Publishing Company, 1985.

Klein, Richard. "Get A Whiff Of This." *The New Republic*, February 6, 1995, 18–23.

Lauder, Estée. *Estée: A Success Story.* New York: Random House, Inc., 1985.

Lefkowith, Christie Mayer. *The Art of Perfume: Discovering and Collecting Perfume Bottles.* New York: Thames and Hudson, Inc., 1994.

Madsen, Axel. *Chanel: A Woman of Her Own.* New York: Henry Holt & Company, Inc., 1990.

Morera, Esther. "Global Fragrance Tastes: The Female Perspective." A report compiled with the American Society of Perfumers for The Fragrance Foundation, September 1995. New York: The Fragrance Foundation, 1995.

Morris, Edwin T. *Fragrance: The Story of Perfume from Cleopatra to Chanel..* New York: Charles Scribner's Sons, 1984.

The New York Times, January 11, 1971, 1, 35. "Chanel, the Couturier, Is Dead in Paris."

" *The Financial Times,* February 25, 1997, 4.

Rawsthorn, Alice. "A Smelling Salt for the Market." *The Financial Times* (London edition), March 11, 1993, 19.

Rubin, David C., Elisabeth Groth, and Debra J. Goldsmith. "Olfactory Cueing of Autobiographical Memory." *American Journal of Psychology,* Winter 1984, 493–507.

Ryan, Kimberley. "Inside Gio's Megalaunch Party." *Women's Wear Daily,* February 5, 1993, 5.

Société Française des Parfumeurs. "Classification des Parfums." Versailles: Société Française des Parfumeurs, 1990.

Société Française des Parfumeurs. "Osmothèque: LaMémoire Vivante des Parfums," Versailles: Société Française des Parfumeurs, 1990.

The New York Times, February 7, 1993, 6. "From Giorgio Armani, by way of Marrakesh."

The New York Times, February 21, 1995, 5 (D). "Champagne Perfume Deal."

Poucher, William A. Revised by G. M. Howard. *Perfumes, Cosmetics & Soaps: Vol. 1, The Raw Materials of Perfumery.* London: Chapman and Hall, 1974.

Poucher, William A. *Perfumes, Cosmetics & Soaps: Vol. 2, The Production, Manufacture and Application of Perfumes.* London: Chapman and Hall, 1974.

Putman, John J. "Napoleon." NATIONAL GEOGRAPHIC, February 1982, 142–189.

Rawsthorn, Alice. "Fragrant Rivals Fail to Outsell No. 5.

Steinhauer, Jennifer. "The Money Department." *The New York Times Magazine.* April 6, 1997, 62–64.

Suskind, Patrick. *Perfume: The Story of a Murderer.* Translated by John E. Woods. London: The Penguin Group, 1986.

Tannen, Mary. "Sex in a Bottle." *The New York Times Magazine,* October 9, 1994, 72–73.

Taylor, Angela. "After That Ad, What Could Tabu Ever Do for an Encore?" *The New York Times,* December 5, 1968, 54.

Vreeland, Diana. *D.V.* New York: Vintage Books, 1985.

Winter, Ruth. *The Smell Book: Scents, Sex, and Society.* Philadelphia and New York: J. P. Lippincott Company, 1976.

GLOSSARY

Source: Adapted and reprinted with the permission of The Fragrance Foundation, 145 East 32nd Street, New York, NY 10016-6002.

Author's Note: While some of these terms do not appear in the text, they are commonly used in the fragrance industry, and the reader may find them of interest.

Absolute, or Absolue in French: A highly concentrated prepared perfumery material usually obtained by alcohol extraction from a concrete. See *Concrete.*

Accord: A balanced complex of three or four notes, which lose their individual identity to create a completely new, unified odor impression. Analogous to the musical terminology in which several notes are combined to create a single chord.

Alcohol: Denatured ethyl alcohol is added to a fragrance compound to serve as the carrier. It modifies the fragrance intensity and makes application to the skin easier. Extract or perfume: 96 proof alcohol combined with oil to a concentration of greater than 22 percent perfume oil. Eau de toilette: 80 or 90 proof alcohol to a concentration of 8 to 15 percent perfume oil. Eau de cologne: 50 to 75 proof alcohol to a concentration of 2 to 5 percent perfume oil.

Aldehyde: An organic chemical that contains a functional group consisting of a carbon, a hydrogen, and an oxygen atom. Aldehydes can be derived from natural or synthetic materials. Aldehydic-type fragrances are characterized by having a rich, opulent top note.

Amaryllis: A bulbous, lily-like plant with umbellate flowers, chiefly native to South America. The oil of amaryllis is often combined with rose and neroli in perfume blends.

Animal-like Notes: Important ingredients such as musk, civet, ambergris, and castoreum were once provided by the animal world exclusively. In modern perfumery, synthetic chemicals mimic virtually all the sensual, heady base notes associated with these scents.

Aroma Chemical: Among the perfumer's primary tools, some synthetic aroma chemicals duplicate chemicals that occur naturally; these are classified as nature-identical aroma chemicals. A second category of aroma chemicals is isolated from natural origins, and a third category consists of the synthetic aroma chemicals not found in nature but that contribute a unique odor value to help broaden a perfumer's library of tools. See *Synthetic Aromatics.*

Attar (Otto): From the Persian for perfume, the term refers to an essential oil obtained by distillation; in particular, that of the Bulgarian rose, an extremely precious perfumery material.

Balance: The result of the blending perfumery components into one harmonious sensory experience.

Balsam: Sticky, resinous material obtained from trees or shrubs that gives a sweet-woody odor associated with well-seasoned, non-coniferous woods such as maple.

Base (Dry Down) Note: Base notes are made up of the underlying tones of the fragrance, and are responsible for its lasting qualities. The ingredients used in base notes are often referred to as fixatives. See *Top Note* and *Middle Note.*

Bayberry: A stocky shrub with grayish berries from which a fragrant wax is extracted. It takes about ten pounds of bayberries to produce one pound of wax, which is used most popularly in candles. Bayberry produces a haunting aroma that is woody and pungent.

Bay Leaf Oil: Distilled from the leaves of a tree grown primarily in the West Indies, and used extensively in masculine fragrances. The aroma of this oil is warm, almost pungent, spicy, and somewhat bitter.

Bergamot: The tangy oil expressed from the nearly ripe, nonedible bergamot orange, which is the size of a large orange and lemon-shaped. The tree is cultivated in the southern part of Calabria, Italy. The fresh, citrus scent of bergamot is important to many fine perfumes, particularly eau de cologne. It is also considered an excellent fixative.

Blend: Any harmonious mixture of fragrance materials.

Blotter Strip (Dip Stick): Pencil-thin, odorless filter paper that is extremely absorbent. It is dipped into raw materials or finished fragrance for sniff-testing by the perfumer or fragrance evaluator. The strip makes it possible to evaluate a small quantity of a material without being overwhelmed.

Body: The main fragrance theme—the "middle" or "heart" of a perfume. Also used to describe a fragrance that is well-rounded or full.

Brief: A description given by a marketer to reflect the type of fragrance to be created by a perfumer. The brief defines the category the prospective fragrance should be in, the type and age of the men and women to whom the scent should appeal, the mood the fragrance should evoke, and the effect it should have on its wearers. It also tells the levels of fragrance desired, and details the bottle, box, color scheme, name, pricing, etc.

Bulgarian Rose: Rosa damascena, grown in Bulgaria's Valley of Roses at the base of the Balkans, produces perhaps the finest rose fragrance in the world. Approximately 4,000 pounds of rose petals are distilled to extract one pound of fragrant oil.

Carnation: A flower cultivated in the south of France that imparts a spicy, clove-like odor to a fragrance. Carnation imbues a fragrance blend with a warm, sensuous note. White carnation flowers are preferred for their more robust scent.

Cedarwood Oil: Distilled from the North American cedar, or the Moroccan juniper. Often used as a base for perfume and men's cologne, it has a woody and tenacious undertone.

Chypre: A blend defined as heavy and clinging with a flowery characteristic. Oakmoss, patchouli, sandalwood, and vetiver are typical of most chypre blends. Other blends may consist of orris, calamus, clary sage, and tarragon. The floral notes are rendered from jasmine, rose, and cassie. Generous additions of citrus oil are required to impart a lift to the fragrance.

Citronella. A grass found in Sri Lanka that renders a colorless or pale yellow oil. The unusually pleasant, warm, woody, yet sweet and fresh odor of citronella oil imparts a brilliant aroma of dewy leaves to fragrances.

Citrus: Oils from lemon, bergamot, lime, tangerine, and bitter orange plants are characterized by a refreshing, tangy scent. Citrus imparts a sharp, clean scent and may be added to a fragrance blend for a top note.

Clary Sage: Distilled from the flowering sage herb grown in southern France, Hungary, and Russia. An aromatic member of the mint family, it tones a scent and reduces a harsh impression by imparting a mellow and sweet note. The oil is often used in eau de cologne.

Clove Buds: The oil and absolute are obtained from the dried flower buds of the slender tropical clove tree found in the Moluccas, especially on the island of Ambon in the eastern Indonesian archipelago. Cultivation of the

Diffusion: The ability of a fragrance to quickly radiate around the wearer.

Distillation: The use of steam in extracting essential oils. Flowers and plants are plunged into water and brought to a boiling point. The resulting steam, which carries the scent, is then cooled. The essential oils are recovered in droplets when the steam is condensed, a process known as decanting. The oily liquids produced have a very strong scent. (One of the six methods of obtaining the essence of natural ingredients; see also: *Expression, Maceration, Enfleurage, Extraction,* and *Headspace Technology.*)

Dry Down: The final phase of a fragrance as it develops on the skin (usually takes 1/2 hour if the skin is dry; less than 15 minutes if skin is oily). Perfumers evaluate the base notes and the tenacity of the fragrance during this stage.

Earthy: The provocative odor of freshly turned earth, musty and rooty.

Enfleurage: One of the oldest methods used to process natural ingredients. Similar to maceration except that cold, purified fats

clove tree dates back at least 2,000 years. The perfumer uses the essence of clove buds to impart a sweet-spicy note to fragrances.

Cologne (Men's): The most concentrated and lasting form of men's fragrance, known in Europe as eau de toilette. A brilliant blend of natural essential oils, aroma chemicals, fixatives, and denatured ethyl alcohol, which acts as the carrier.

Cologne (Women's): Usually the lightest form of fragrance, it may be used lavishly as an after-bath refresher. Introduced in the city of Cologne, Germany, in the 17th century, it was the first citrus fragrance; the word is derived from "eau de Cologne," meaning water of Cologne. It was often combined with lavender notes. Eau de cologne still enjoys its popularity, but today cologne also connotes a lighter concentration of perfume.

Concrete: Solid, waxy substance representing the closest odor duplication of the flower, bark, leaves, etc., from which it has been extracted. Concrete can be further concentrated to produce absolute.

Cool: Describes outdoor scents such as green leaves, fresh flowers, bracing mint notes, and citrus.

Costus: A large plant with roots that render a fragrant oil. Costus oil smooths the violet note in a fragrance blend, imparts a warm and unique note to oriental blends, and complements vetiver, sandalwood, patchouli, and geranium.

are used rather than hot ones. As in maceration, a pomade is formed, then washed with alcohol; from this an extract of flower oil is obtained. Enfleurage is a labor-intensive process, making the cost prohibitive in modern perfumery. This method, however, produces the very finest jasmine and tuberose oils. (One of the six methods of obtaining the essence of natural ingredients; see also: *Expression, Macertion, Distillation, Extraction,* and *Headspace Technology.*)

Environmental Fragrance: Fragrance introduced into the surroundings for pleasure or to enhance a sense of well-being, increase alertness, or to provide a relaxing environment. These fragrance forms include, among others, fragrance diffusers, scented candles, potpourri, sachets, pomanders, shelf liners, scent burners, and sprays.

Essential Oil: The fragrant, volatile extracts ob-tained from flowers, grass, stems, seeds, leaves, roots, bark, fruits, tree moss, and tree secretions. Essential oils are the basic ingredients employed by the perfumer, and are obtained by various means. See *Distillation, Expression, Extraction, Enfleurage, Maceration,* and *Headspace Technology.*

Evaporation: The process of changing from a liquid to a vapor. To slow down the evaporation process after a perfume bottle has been opened, the stopper should be closed tightly and the bottle stored in its box in a cool place.

Expression: A method used to extract oils from citrus fruits. Expression simply means pressing out the oils from fruits that have a scented substance in their rind. They are pressed using of modern, hydraulic presses. (The simplest of the six methods of obtaining the essence of natural ingredients; see also: *Enfleurage, Maceration, Distillation, Extraction, and Headspace Technology.*)

Extract: Concentrated perfume or flower product obtained through the extraction process using volatile solvents.

Extraction (with volatile solvents): The most commonly used and effective method of obtaining the oils of fragrant ingredients, though very expensive. Plant materials are added to volatile solvents, such as petroleum ether or benzene, at a low temperature. As the solvents flow over the plants in sealed containers, the oils are released without the use of harmful heat. The solvent is then evaporated to obtain the concrete—a strongly scented, waxy substance. The concrete is then mixed with alcohol, agitated, filtered, and frozen. The alcohol is allowed to evaporate, yielding absolute. (One of the

basic families: *Aldehyde, Citrus, Floral Bouquet, Fruity, Green, Oriental, Single Floral, Spicy, and Woody-Mossy.*

Frangipani: A perfume named after an illustrious 11th-century Roman family. Originally used in scented gloves, the jasmine-like scent is blended by the perfumer, with a variety of spices and aroma chemicals, allowing the sweet, smooth jasmine-like note to dominate.

Frankincense: See *olibanum.*

Fresh: An invigorating, outdoor, nature-inspired fragrance with green and/or citrus notes.

Fruity: The impression of full, ripe, edible fruit odors (excluding citrus) within the fragrance theme.

six methods of obtaining the essence of natural ingredients; see also: *Enfleurage, Maceration, Distillation, Expression, and Headspace Technology.*)

Factice (Dummy): A regular or oversized display perfume flacon that contains tinted liquid instead of fragrance.

Fixative: A fragrance ingredient that prolongs the continuity and life of the odor. Vital to the creation of fragrance, fixatives modify the evaporation rate of all note-giving elements. Derived most often from mosses, resins, and aroma chemicals, they may be an essential ingredient of the bouquet, or an important blender.

Flacon: An artistically-designed perfume bottle. It is usually topped with an ornamental stopper designed to keep the flacon airtight.

Floral Bouquet: A fragrance composition based on a combination of floral notes. The major components of this family of fragrances are rose, jasmine, gardenia, and carnation, as well as such favorites as lily of the valley and lilac.

Fougère: The French word for fern. Fougère fragrances depend on aromatic chemicals to produce the fern-like notes that combine well with lavender, citrus, and coumarin in fragrances for men.

Fragrance: In perfumery terminology, a general term for any concentration, such as perfume, eau de parfum, eau de toilette, or cologne.

Fragrance Family: Fragrances that are constructed in a similar manner and have key ingredient combinations in common are said to be in the same family. Even though each fragrance within a family has its own personality, it usually shares middle and base notes with other fragrances. See individual listings for each of the following

Full-Bodied: A fragrance with harmonious accords that renders a rich, robust scent.

Fungal: Odors suggestive of molds, mushrooms, and fungi. Important notes in muguet fragrances, as well as other florals.

Galbanum: A gum resin, yellow/brown in color, that contains a pleasing, aromatic, volative oil. It is an essentially "green" smell (see *Green Note*).

Gardenia: The rich, heavy odor of gardenia absolute is a precious ingredient to the perfumer. The essence is too overpowering to be used alone in a fragrance, and is therefore softened with more delicate notes. One ton of blossoms renders less than one pound of fragrant oil.

Gas Chromatography/Mass Spectrometry: The laboratory technique most commonly used in fragrance analysis. It is used routinely in quality control to identify and ensure consistency of the fragrance from one production to the next.

Genealogy of Fragrance: The classification of fragrance families by odor type, such as floral, citrus, chypre, leather, and fantasy notes, that owe their characteristics to their famous fragrance ancestors and have a family history or genealogy. Major innovations and departures from traditional odor types can spawn a whole new classification to add to the fragrance family tree. See *Fragrance Family*.

Geranium: Cultivated in the south of France, Spain, Russia, North Africa, and Egypt, the oil from geranium leaves and stems is one of the most important essential oils used in fine perfumes and soaps. The oil imparts a sweet, rosy odor that blends well with rose and oriental notes and lends a rich, robust character. Approximately 200,000 pounds of oil are produced annually.

Ginger: Oil of ginger is distilled from the rhizomes of the ginger plant grown in Jamaica, Africa, India, China, and Japan. Warm and pungently spicy, it adds flair to oriental and modern blends.

Grasse: A town near the coast of southern France, once known as the world capital of perfumery. It was famous for its abundance of flowers used in the creation of fragrances.

Green Note: Usually the top note of a fragrance composition that evokes the zest and energy of freshly cut grass and dewy green leaves. Green notes add lift and create a young, vigorous mood in a fragrance.

Gum: Resinous substance exuded from the bark, twigs, or leaves of trees or shrubs. Includes resin and balsam.

Harmonious: A term used by the perfumer to express order, accord, and unity in a fragrance.

Hyacinth: A member of the lily family, with blue, white, pink, or purple flowers, that grows wild among the olive groves of Grasse. The hyacinth flower releases a delicate fragrance just as it appears on the plant. The odor of hyacinth oil, when diluted, assumes a smooth, sweet, yet powerful scent.

Incense: Fragrant gums and resins in powder or solid form that are burned to give off a lingering, scented smoke. It is the original form in which fragrance was used.

Infusion / Tincture: A solution obtained by prolonged contact with alcohol. When hot alcohols are used, it is called an infusion. When the alcohols are at room temperature or warm, the solution is called a tincture.

Ionone: One of the most valued synthesized products used by the

Headspace Technology: A relatively new form of analysis that uses gas chromatography/mass spectrometry to yield a fingerprint (see *Smell Fingerprint*) of odors in the air. The technique is often used to reproduce the aroma of living plants, flowers, fruits, and herbs. (One of the six methods of obtaining the essence of natural ingredients; see also: *Enfleurage, Maceration, Distillation, Expression, and Extraction.*)

Heady: A fragrance with a powerful, intoxicating appeal.

Heat: Added energy that causes substances to undergo change. Heat expands and intensifies fragrance.

Herb: A plant or parts of a plant that may have therapeutic qualities.

Herbaceous: A fragrance note that is grassy green, spicy, and thought to be therapeutic, e.g., thyme, hyssop, chamomile.

Herbal: A broad spectrum of odor characteristics—from the green, camphoraceous notes such as cardamon, sage, and thyme to the slightly spicy herbal note of basil and the minty cooling notes of peppermint and spearmint.

Herbal Green: All of the characteristics of herbal notes with additional leafy and/or grassy green notes. The additional leafy green notes can be attained through the use of essential oils or synthetic chemicals to impart a more natural impression.

Honey: A very sweet, heavy, syrupy, tenacious fragrance note.

Honeysuckle: A well-known vine with tiny, very fragrant flowers. The essence of honeysuckle is usually created with various floral scents of natural or synthetic origin.

perfumer, it is essential to violet perfumes. It is used in small amounts in floral, woody, and herbaceous perfumes.

Jasmine: A delicate white flower from which one of the most vital of essential oils is extracted. Even a minute quantity of this potent oil will impart smoothness and energy to fine fragrances. A pound of jasmine absolute typically costs about a thousand dollars. There are over 200 species of jasmine that are indigenous to southern Europe, Asia, and Africa, although it was cultivated in France. It must be picked by hand in early morning, or it will lose much of its fragrance value. It takes 1,300 pounds of the delicate, white flowers to produce two pounds of absolute.

Labdanum: A gummy substance obtained from certain varieties of the rockrose (a perennial herb that grows wild all over the United States) that imparts a leathery note to perfume. One of the methods used to collect the labdanum resin is to comb the material from beards of goats and fleece of sheep that have come in contact with the foliage.

Lasting Quality: The ability of a fragrance to retain its character on the skin. See *Substantivity.*

Lavandin: A hybrid plant developed by crossing true lavender with spike or aspic lavender. Lavandin constitutes one of the largest volumes of natural fragrance materials, and is grown on expansive plantations in France and northern Africa.

Lavender: A low-growing evergreen plant with a pale purple flowering top, native to Mediterranean countries. The top and stalks are steam-distilled to extract the fresh, sweet oil used in citrus colognes and lavender water, as well as in fougères, chypres, and florals.

Leather: Fragrance type and odor resembling the sweet, pungent, smoky characteristic of tanned leathers. Identified as a masculine note, the perfumer often re-creates the leather odor by using oil of birch tar and various aromatic chemicals.

Lemongrass: A grass found primarily in the East Indies, Madagascar, and Brazil. It is distilled to produce the oil of lemongrass, which is used to scent soaps and bath salts.

Lemon Oil: An expressed oil from the almost ripe rinds of the fruit from a special variety of lemon tree. Lemon oil is refreshing and slightly sharp. It is used as a top note in countless perfume types.

Light: A fragrance with a predominant fresh note. Often formulated as a deodorant cologne for all-over body wear in warm climates or for sports.

of the fragrance ingredients. In the heart of the fragrance, the dominant notes will serve to classify the fragrance family—floral, chypre, green, spicy, oriental. It usually takes about ten minutes for the middle or heart notes to fully develop on the skin. See *Top Note* and *Base Note.*

Mimosa: The plant is native to Australia and was cultivated in France by around 1820. The flower and twig ends are harvested in the very early spring. The extract from the flower radiates a delicate waxy-sweet undertone. Mimosa adds smoothness to a fragrance and its fixative value is outstanding.

Mossy: An odor suggestive of the aromatic lichens and mosses, primarily oakmoss and tree moss; reminiscent of forest depths. Although the overall odor of mosses can be singularly defined, each oil bears a distinct scent.

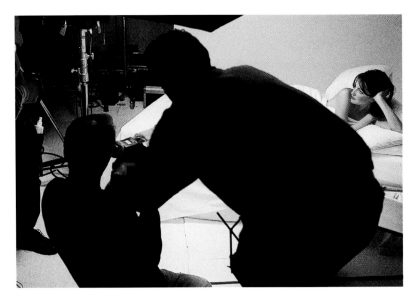

Lilac: The oil extracted from the lilac does not accurately represent the fragrance exuded by the flower. The perfumer uses aromatic chemicals to achieve lilac notes.

Limbic System: The area of the brain that receives and interprets the fragrance message from the olfactory nerves. Located deep inside the brain, the limbic system is the seat of our emotions, creativity, sexuality, and memory.

Maceration: A process by which flowers are steeped in vats of hot fats. Maceration forms pomades, which are then washed in alcohol to purify the scented mixture so that an extract of flower oil can be obtained (very similar to enfleurage). This expensive process requires a lot of hand labor. (One of the six methods of obtaining the essence of natural ingredients; see also: *Enfleurage, Expression, Distillation, Extraction, and Headspace Technology.*)

Magnolia: The flamboyant and delightfully fragrant flowers of the magnolia tree found in North America, China, and Japan render almost none of the oil used commercially in the creation of perfume. A blend of jasmine, neroli, rose, ylang-ylang, and a variety of aromatic chemicals impart a full-bodied, sweet bouquet, suggesting the magnolia fragrance.

Mellow: As in wine and music, a mellow fragrance is one that has achieved a perfect balance, assuring a smooth, rich impression.

Micro-encapsulation: A technique of incorporating fragrance oil into a solid, thin-walled capsule. Release of the oil is generally achieved by breaking the capsule walls. Common uses include scratch and sniff, fragrance samplers, and dry perfume.

Middle Notes: Also called the heart notes, they are a harmonious blend

Muguet: The sweet fragrance of *muguet,* also known as lily of the valley, is re-created with aroma chemicals and enhanced by ylang-ylang, orange blossoms, jasmine, and rose oils. The yield of oil obtained from the flower is minimal, and therefore seldom used.

Narcissus: The unusual scent of these fragile yellow-and-white flowers make them an expensive and much sought-after perfume ingredient. May be rounded with natural floral notes or aroma chemicals.

Neroli Oil: A distillate prepared from the blossoms of either the sweet or bitter orange tree. Neroli oil is light and imparts sweetness and evanescence to a fragrance blend.

Night Bloomer: Certain flowers, such as honeysuckle, jasmine, and evening primrose bloom at night. Night bloomers are light in color and very fragrant, and therefore can be located easily by their nocturnal pollinators.

Nose: A vernacular expression for a perfumer. See *Perfumer.*

Note: Borrowed from the language of music to indicate an olfactory impression of a single smell, or to indicate the three parts of a perfume: top, middle, and base notes.

Nutmeg: The seed enveloped in the fruit of the nutmeg tree, which grows in many tropical climates. The unusually pleasing odor is often used in lavender water. Sometimes used to impart a spicy quality to tobacco.

Oakmoss: A fixative extracted from fragrant lichen collected from oaks and other tree species of Yugoslavia, Tuscany, and southern France. Often used in heavy bouquets, oakmoss imparts an earthy note to perfumes.

Oceanic: A synthetically produced fragrance component of modern perfumery that evokes ocean-like qualities.

Odor: Airborne chemicals that stimulate the olfactory system. They emanate from objects, perfumes, etc., and constitute the characteristic smell of something.

Odor Fatigue: The inability to distinguish a particular odor as the receptors in the upper nose become desensitized. A different scent introduced into a person's olfactory system, however, can still be perceived. When testing fragrances, no more than three should be tried at any one time.

Odor Memory: The sense of smell, more than any of our other senses, influences our ability to recall past events and experience. Fragrance is considered one of the most potent mediums for conjuring up a memory. See also *Limbic System.*

from India by Arab traders and ia a traditional symbol of fertility in a marriage. Grown in the sunny climates of Florida, California, Sicily, and Spain, the extract from the delicate blossoms yields an especially full, ambrosial note.

Orange Oil: Expressed from peels of both bitter and sweet oranges.

Organ: A unit once basic to the perfumer, consisting of a series of semicircular stepped shelves lined with hundreds of bottles of raw perfume materials arranged by scent category. Sitting at the organ, the perfumer could construct fragrance creations in much the same way as a musician chooses musical notes and chords.

Oriental: Sophisticated, mysterious, and sultry, this uninhibited fragrance type is achieved through a blending of brilliant, exotic flowers, herbs, and fixatives. It is designed to have a strong erotic appeal.

Oleoresin: Either a natural or prepared material. Natural oleo-resins are exudations from tree-trunks, barks, etc. Prepared oleo-resins are liquid preparations, extracted from botanicals with solvents that can extract oil and resinous matter from the botanical, yielding the oleo-resin as evaporation residue.

Olibanum (Frankincense): A gum resin from a tree found in Arabia and eastern Africa. Olibanum is used most often in oriental blends, and is noted for its extraordinary fixative properties. It is also used in face powders and soaps.

Olfactory: Relating to, or connected with, the sense of smell.

Olfactory Bulb: The first region of the brain to receive sensory input from the olfactory epithelium. The olfactory bulb receives the initial input and communicates with numerous other regions of the brain, e.g., the hypothalamus and cortex, via the limbic system.

Olfactory Detection Threshold: The lowest concentration of a vapor that can be identified as different from a background stimulus.

Olfactory Epithelium: Layer of sensory cells in the upper rear portion of the nose. Each side of the nose contains millions of sensory cells in the epithelium.

Olfactory Recognition Threshold: The lowest concentration of a vapor that can be recognized appropriately.

Opoponax: An essential oil from the gum resin of a tree belonging to the same genus as the one that produces myrrh. It is an excellent fixative, sweet with woody undertones. It replaces many natural animal notes.

Orange Blossom: The classic fragrance of the orange flower was brought

Orris Absolute: Produced from orris concrete, which is derived from the rhizome of the iris plant, this is the most expensive of all natural perfume materials—$40,000 a pound.

Oxidation: The chemical change or alteration of fragrance due to exposure to air.

Ozone: A synthetically produced fragrance note of modern perfumery that evokes pure, clean, and refreshing qualities.

Palette: The hundreds of fragrance raw materials from which the perfumer selects those needed for a particular fragrance creation.

Patchouli: The oil thatis derived from a leaf grown in India, Malaysia, Indonesia, and South America. Patchouli, an excellent fixative, provides a musty, exotic note to perfume blends and is often an important ingredient in oriental blends. In recent years patchouli has become a fragrance form in itself and is usually used in conjunction with vetiver. In its raw state, the patchouli leaf exudes an odor reminiscent of wet wood and rusty iron. The essential oilmis burnt-orange or brownish in color, and possesses a sweet, herbaceous, spicy, and woody-balsamic odor.

Perfume: The most concentrated, strongest, and longest-lasting of fragrance forms, it is a brilliant blend that may contain several hundred ingredients. The word can be traced to the Latin words *per,* of, and *fumare,* to smoke.

Perfumer: Often referred to as the nose, the perfumer has an innate artistic and imaginative sense, as well as a highly developed sense of smell. It takes many years of training for the perfumer to perfect the olfactory memory that will allow him or her to not only recognize many hundreds of raw materials, but to recall innumerable beautiful harmonies and blends. The perfumer, who usually serves as an apprentice for a minimum of six years, must have the rare creative ability to visualize a scent and "construct" it using the olfactory memory, just as an artist draws upon memory of color and form; a wine expert upon recall of the type of grape, vintage, and locale of a particular wine; and a musician upon musical repertoire and fundamental structure of music, harmonies, etc.

Petitgrain: The oil, distilled from the leaves and the twigs of the bitter orange tree, imparts a mellow note to colognes and toilet waters. It is often used in conjunction with lemon and orange. Although found in South America and North Africa, the best petitgrain is cultivated in the south of France.

Pheromone: A chemical substance secreted by an animal or insect for the purpose of influencing the behavior of others from their own or

Rhizome: A root-like stem with buds, nodes, and scale-like leaves that grows under or along the ground. It is the part of the plant from which certain raw perfume materials are derived, including orris absolute and ginger oil.

Rich: A term applied to a fragrance that possesses a depth and harmony intensified by a mellow tone and full-bodied quality.

Rose: One of the most valued ingredients in perfumery, the rose fragrance is rich and clinging. The many varieties of roses offer a wide palette of fragrances to the perfumer. The "essence" of roses varies from fruity to violet-like, while still others possess hints of the warmth and depth of musk and myrrh.

Rose de Mai: The deep, rosy, rich absolute from this rose, grown primarily in the south of France, is a very important perfume raw

different species. Pheromones may be produced as sexual attractants, to mark a trail, or to give information of a specific type.

Pomade: A combination of purified fats and flower oils that is the result of the processes of enfleurage and maceration.

Pomander: A perforated, decorative box or ball that contains an assortment of dried flower petals, roots, leaves, spices, and essential oils.

Potpourri: An aromatic mingling of dry or moist flower petals, roots, leaves, spices, and essential oils in a variety of forms, including pomander balls and sachets. Potpourri is often presented in jars, baskets, bags, boxes, pillows, hangers, and decorative objects.

Powdery: Usually applies to a scent that expresses a sweet, dry, and musky character.

Receptor Cell: Located in the olfactory epithelium, each cell has microscopic hairs (cilia) extending into the mucus. Odor molecules are thought to bind chemically to specific sites on these cilia. This chemical event is translated into an electrical message that is transmitted to the olfactory bulb.

Resin: Solid or semisolid gums derived from trees, particularly pine and other evergreens. Resins are noted for their fixative properties.

Resinoid: An extraction of gums, balsams, resins, or roots (orris) that consist in whole or in part of resinous materials. They are generally used as fixatives in perfume compositions.

Retronasal Olfaction: Stimulation of the olfactory receptor cells by odors that originate in our mouth (most often during eating) and travel to the olfactory epithelium during exhalation.

material. Rich, diffusive, and tenacious, *rose de mai* rounds off and lifts many perfume compositions.

Rosemary: An aromatic herb in the mint family, it has light blue flowers. The brilliantly refreshing scent distilled from the leaves is used in eau de colognes and other fragrance blends to impart a vigor and briskness.

Rosewood Oil: Oil distilled from the wood of a tree grown in South America, used in aromatic blends, especially rose compounds.

Round: A fine fragrance blend is refined until perfect balance and harmony are achieved. Once the composition is rich and mellow, smooth and perfectly toned, the fragrance is considered to be round.

Sandalwood: The oil is distilled from the coarse, powdered wood and roots of the small tree grown in India and Australia. In India the tree is government-controlled. Used in sacred rituals as far back as the year 500 B.C., sandalwood is still a part of Indian and Chinese religious ceremonies. It has a woody, balsamic note and is of great fixative value.

Sillage: The fragrance aura perceived after an individual wearing a perfume has passed.

Single Floral: These fragrances have the recognizable scent of a single flower, although this impression may be created with numerous ingredients.

Skin Chemistry: The chemical behavior of the skin varies from individual to individual and is influenced by variables such as diet, skin type, environment, and medication. The skin can modify fragrance character, and as a result, a particular fragrance will smell different depending upon who is wearing it.

Smell Fingerprint: The individual characteristics of a fragrance creation as it develops on skin (see also *Skin Chemistry*) and as it is portrayed by analysis (see *Gas Chromatography/Mass Spectrometry*).

Solvent: A fluid used to extract the essential oils from herbs, flowers, fruits, resins, and other natural perfumery materials.

Specialties: Natural oils, natural isolates, or synthetics, either alone or in combination, that are used as building blocks for fragrance compounds. They are less complex than a finished fragrance compound. They may be an end product of special processing treatments or unique raw materials, and are usually supplied by a single company under a trade name.

Spices / Herbs: See individual entries for the most popular varieties: *Bayberry, Bay Leaf, Clary Sage, Clove, Costus, Ginger, Lavender, Nutmeg, Rosemary, Thyme,* and *Vanilla.*

Spicy: Piquant or pungent notes such as clove oil and cinnamon; characteristic of notes such as carnation, ginger, and lavender, and the chemical spicy notes. Because certain spices yield their scents in such minute quantities, the perfumer may re-create them with chemicals.

Stability: A reasonable length of time for a fragrance to remain stable before the product is affected by heat, light, and air. Once a bottle of perfume is opened, it is meant to be used, otherwise it will begin to fade with time. Long exposure to strong sunlight or extremes in temperature, particularly heat, can disturb the delicate balance of the perfume and change its color and scent. To last, perfume should be kept tightly closed in a cool, dry place away from direct light.

Storax (Styrax): A balsam from a tree of Asia Minor. The odor is similar to naphtha and when refined and used sparingly, it resembles a bouquet of hyacinth, tuberose, and jonquil.

Strength: The intensity of a fragrance in any of its many forms, e.g., perfume, eau de parfum, eau de toilette, and cologne.

Substantivity: The lastingness of a perfume after it has been applied to the skin.

Sweet: Can be used to describe a fragrance that has richness and ambrosial characteristics associated with sweet taste.

Sweet Pea: A popular garden flower with climbing vines. A typical characteristic of the sweet pea scent is its suave lightness; it is used in floral, sweet, and light perfume bases to be blended and modified with other perfume bases.

Synergism: The ability of certain perfumery ingredients to work together to produce an effect greater than the ingredients could achieve independently.

Synthetic Aromatics: May be derived or isolated from nature or synthesized in the laboratory. Some aroma chemicals are superior to natural ones in uniformity, stability, and availability.

Tenacity: The ability of a perfume to last, or a fragrance note to retain its characteristic odor.

Tester: Fragrance spray bottle, or a specially designed container, provided by most fragrance companies, to allow the customer to try a scent directly on the skin.

Thin: Lacking in body and depth. Occurs when a fragrance complex has not been given enough "floralcy" or warmth to soften the impact of the more aggressive and volatile components.

Thyme: Aromatic and known for its pine-like vigor, this herb is grown several thousand feet up in the mountains along the Mediterranean. Small amounts of thyme impart a refreshing scent to many eau de colognes.

Tincture: Alcoholic extracts of natural raw materials; the solvent is left in the extract as a diluent. A tincture is a prepared perfumery or flavor material.

Tobacco: Dry and mossy-balsamic nuance used in men's fragrances, creating the impression of dried, cured tobacco. Perfumers use extract from real tobacco, as well as notes of aroma chemical origin.

Toilet Water (Eau de Toilette): Less concentrated than perfume or eau de parfum. It is created with fragrance oil at a lighter concentration to make it more subtle. Toilet water is the ideal all-over-the-body base for a perfume application.

Tonality: The theme that communicates the mood of the fragrance.

Tone: The quality of fragrance components, that, when blended together, create the tonality or ambience of a fragrance.

Top Note: The first scent impression of a fragrance after the bottle has been opened and immediately after it has been applied to the skin. Designed by the perfumer to be ephemeral and volatile, it sets the sensory stage for the development of middle and base notes, which provide the final impression of the fragrance as they all meld together on the skin. See *Middle Note* and *Base Note.*

Tuberose: A member of the lily family, the tuberose flower possesses a scent atypical of its family origin. When added to a fragrance, it enriches and adds depth. The sensuous, fragrant oil, once obtained by enfleurage, enhances the notes of gardenia, narcissus, hyacinth, and jonquil. It is one of the most expensive of the essential oils.
Undertone: The subtle nuance of the fragrance background.

Vanilla: The fruit or seeds of a climbing orchid native to tropical America, it provides the essence that adds richness and depth to many sweet-floral or amber bases. The tenacity of vanilla is outstanding.

Velvety: A soft, smooth, mellow fragrance.

Vetiver: A grass with heavy, fibrous roots that grows in the warm climates of Haiti, Réunion, and India. The rhizomes are distilled to produce a rich oil. The odor echoes the scent of moist earth and roots with rich undertones of wood. Vetiver, an excellent fixative, imparts a dry, spirited tone to chypre and fougère blends.

Violet: The extraction of the oils of the violet is difficult and extremely costly, since an entire acre of the tiny flowers, grown in the cool shade of the olive and citrus trees of southern France, produces only a few drops. Aroma chemicals allow this precious scent to be enjoyed by all.

Volatile: The property of being diffused freely in the atmosphere; easily vaporized at a low temperature.

Warm: An ample scent that generates emotional warmth and conveys a sensation of intimacy and well-being.

Woody-Mossy: Sandalwood, rosewood, cedar, and other aromatic woods are combined with earthy oakmoss and fern notes to create fragrance types refreshingly foresty, clean, clear, and crisp.

Woody: An essence reminiscent of the aroma of freshly cut wood and roots dried under the sun. The perfumer achieves a woody effect with ingredients such as sandalwood and vetiver.

Ylang-ylang: Literally translated "flower of flowers," the blossom of the ylang-ylang tree, which can attain the height of 60 feet, is grown in Madagascar, the Philippines, and the Comoros. The flower is greenish-yellow, with a red center, and grows in clusters of three to four. The distilled flower oil is rich, sweet, and rather balsamic, and adds a "lift" to oriental blends. Ylang-ylang softens and rounds harsh notes in a fragrance composition and blends well with jasmine and violet.

CREDITS

All photographs are by Robb Kendrick with the exception of the following:

Sam Abell, National Geographic photographer: 2, 43; Lynn Abercrombie: 20, 26, 29, 31; Thomas J. Abercrombie: 28; 1934 photo by Cecil Beaton: 133; Bijan: 141, 143; CHANEL, 137; Cotton Coulson: 44 (top left); Dana Perfumes: 117 (left); Estée Lauder Companies: 118; Givaudan Roure: 13 (bottom), 86–87, 89, 95, 100; Photos by HATAMI copyright CHANEL: 134, 135, 139; Lauros-Giraudon/Bridgeman Art Library, London/New York: 24–25; The Granger Collection, New York: 38; Sheila Metzner: 117 (right); Eric T. Michelson: 10; James L. Stanfield: 23; Susan Stillman: 12; Maggie Steber: 108–109, 110, 153; Brooks Walker: 1, 40, 65, 126, 155: Copyright 1998 Andy Warhol Foundation for the Visual Arts/ARS, New York: 130.

CAPTIONS FOR FRONT AND BACK MATTER

ii–iii Lavender fields in France; iv–v Memorizing scents at the Givaudan Roure perfume school in Grasse, France; vi–vii Angie Battaglia of Austin, Texas applies a favorite fragrance; viii Lavender in France; ix Obelisk-shaped bottle for Ramses II perfume, 1928; x–xi Jasmine picker in India; xii Roses in Bulgaria; xiii Bottle for C'est by Silka, 1920; 144–145 A cavalcade of contemporary fragrances; 147 Fields of French lavender; 149 Fields of French lavender; 150 Chopping sandalwood in India; 151 Hauling sandalwood logs to be processed; 152 Photographer Herb Ritts directs the shooting of an Allure ad; 153 New York City launch party for Flirt by Prescriptives; 154 Fragrance testing at International Flavors & Fragrances, New York City; 157 An auction of antique perfume bottles in Geneva, Switzerland; 158 A rose picker sniffs a bloom in Bulgaria.

Published by THE NATIONAL GEOGRAPHIC SOCIETY

John M. Fahey, Jr. President and Chief Executive Officer
Gilbert M. Grosvenor Chairman of the Board
Nina D. Hoffman Senior Vice President
William R. Gray Vice President and Director, Book Division
Charles Kogod Assistant Director
Barbara A. Payne Editorial Director and Managing Editor
David Griffin Design Director
R. Gary Colbert Production Director
Dale-Marie Herring Assistant Editor
Lewis R. Bassford Production Project Manager
Heidi Splete Editorial Assistant
Judith Bell, Susan O'Keefe Researchers

MANUFACTURING AND QUALITY MANAGEMENT
George V. White Director
John T. Dunn Associate Director
Vincent P. Ryan Manager
Polly P. Tompkins Executive Assistant

Prepared for THE NATIONAL GEOGRAPHIC SOCIETY by
Coleen O'Shea Literary Enterprises Project Director
Barbara Cohen Aronica Book Designer
Diane Shanley Copyeditor

A C K N O W L E D G M E N T S

A book, like a perfume, is a collaborative effort—impossible without the creative energy and support of many. Nina Hoffman, senior vice president of the National Geographic Society, saw the possibility of the book in a magazine story, and William L. Allen and Robert M. Poole, editor and associate editor respectively, of the National Geographic, allowed me the time to write it. Appreciation is also due to my editor on the book, Coleen O'Shea, who helped me expand into and embrace the space a book allowed, and for measuring out tactful suggestion, encouragement, and good humor in just the right doses.

For the gift of candor, knowledge, and time, I am particularly grateful to the following people: Yves de Chiris of Quest provided hours of wisdom, wit, and wonderful conversation. Patrick Firmenich of Firmenich suggested the idea for the Cathy perfume; Cathleen Montrose and her staff made it happen. Ann Gottlieb of Ann Gottlieb Associates generously allowed for wide-ranging inquiries into the nature of the fragrance business and the impulses that drive it. Sally Yeh of Bijan Fragrances lifted the curtain so I might witness the creation and launch of a new fragrance. Geoffrey Webster of Givaudan Roure opened countless doors and made things happen. Tom McGee and Ken Purzycki, also of Givaudan Roure, guided me through the jungles of Costa Rica and organic chemistry. Françoise Marin, formerly of Givaudan Roure, taught me to love French jasmine nearly as much as she does. For special insights I am indebted to: Annette Green of the Fragrance Foundation; Pete Born of *Women's Wear Daily*; John Ledes and Adelaide Farah of *Beauty Fashion*; André Gerber of the Osmothèque; Timra Carlson of NPD Beauty *Trends*; Dr. Luca Turin; Véra Strübi of Thierry Mugler Parfums; Chantal

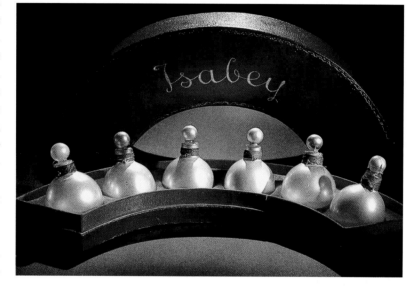

Roos of Beauté Prestige International; Annick Goutal of Annick Goutal; Allan Mottus of Allan Mottus Associates; Olwen Wolfe of Olwen Wolfe and Associates; and Serge Lutens. I am also indebted to: Véronique de Pardieu, Marie-Louise de Clermont-Tonnerre, Jacques Polge, Pierre Buntz, Jacques Helleu, Claire Chassard, Marika Genty, Susan Duffy, Lauri Palma, all of Chanel. Paul Austin and Shirley Giovetti of Quest; Sheila Hewett of Calvin Klein; Leonard Lauder, Evelyn Lauder, and Jeanette Wagner of the Estée Lauder Companies; as well as Karyn Khoury, also with Lauder, who understands that in the end it's the beauty of what's in the bottle that matters.

Annie Buzantian, Harry Frémont, James Krivda, Ilias Ermenidis, and Thierry Wasser of Firmenich; Steve De Mercado, James Bell, and Kari Ariente of Givaudan Roure; Rodrigo Flores-Roux and Claude Dir of Quest; Jean Kerleo of Jean Patou; Koi-chi Shiozawa of Aveda; Sophia Grojsman of IFF, all allowed me glimpses into the perfumer's head and heart. How much I admire and respect their work. In Paris, my friend Claudine Ripert always snagged and set up the impossible interview. Dominique Goby led the way in Morocco. Caroline Mitchell and Moira Tulloch interpreted for me in France. Thanks to my colleagues on the magazine who helped on this project and encouraged me in many ways: Jennifer Reek, Elizabeth Cheng Krist, Mary McPeak, Connie Phelps, Sisse Brimberg, Kathy Moran, Betty Clayman-DeAtley, and Sandy Sidey, in Paris. Special thanks to my assistant, Heidi Splete, for tirelessly keeping all the bits and pieces together. And deep appreciation to the writer's allies—researchers Susan O'Keefe and Judith Bell.